The Relationship Marketer

Søren Hougaard
Mogens Bjerre

The Relationship Marketer

Rethinking Strategic Relationship Marketing

Second Edition

 Springer

Søren Hougaard
Loevvaenget 3
2960 Rungsted Kyst
Denmark
shougaard@amsgroup.dk

Mogens Bjerre
Solbjerg Plads 3
2000 Frederiksberg
Denmark
mogens.bjerre@cbs.dk

Co-publication by Springer-Verlag, Heidelberg, Germany
and Samfundslitteratur, Frederiksberg, Denmark

First edition published 2002 as "Strategic Relationship Marketing"

This edition is for countries outside of Scandinavia.
Please order the book from Springer-Verlag: www.springer.com.

For orders from Scandinavia please order the book from Samfundslitteratur Press:
www.samfundslitteratur.dk

ISBN 978-3-642-03242-4   e-ISBN 978-3-642-03243-1
DOI 10.1007/978-3-642-03243-1
Springer Heidelberg Dordrecht London New York

[Dyad: the principle of twoness or "you and me". Dyadic thinking seeks to understand the relationship and dynamics between two parties acting in complex network contexts. Dyad marketing is the basic principle according to which the strategic marketer focuses on the customer relationship and the benefits of mutuality.]

Contents

Welcome to the fantastic universe of relationships and strategic relationship marketing!

Our vision is to take you, our reader, on an exciting journey to the borderland of dyad marketing management based on a relationship-oriented understanding of business life. This ambition is far-reaching in the sense that we intend to present and develop a marketing philosophy that is – to some extent – new and unconditionally focused on dyad marketing relationships. Furthermore, we aim at offering a relationship approach to strategy which is both theoretically founded and applicable in real life situations. Indeed not a low ambition.

Many well-established management theories, we believe, need to be reformulated, as the network economy sweeps through business life and influences all corners of society. Individuals and groups will behave in new ways; organisations will become reconfigured and will have to develop new cooperative and adaptive mechanisms to stay competitive. All that can think must link.

The importance of strategic and marketing excellence to obtain outstanding performance remains unchanged. But a great many aspects of strategic marketing do change as you take on the dyadic perspective.

The Dawn of Dyad Marketing Thinking

So, the demand for a relationship-based dyad marketing framework is growing. Structures and conditions of markets have changed. Competition moves away from inter-firm rivalry to competition among value chains leading us in a direction of *dyadic* or even triadic marketing management. Any company must therefore pay attention to the supply chain as a vertical system and try to create relationship benefits for customers and suppliers, not just for the company itself.

Industries, where relationships between trade parties are a critical success factor – e.g. within services, information technology, new media and telecommunications are gaining momentum in the global economy at a tremendous speed. In many situations time-to-market, capacity, trust and stability are a competitive necessity, whereas price seems to be a much less important issue. Partnership – and not arms' length business practice – is on the marketing agenda.

At all levels of society, BtB as well as BtC, interactivity is a fact. Before the age of interactivity and the indefinite access to information, marketing decisions were governed by the *economics of things*[4]. Management faced a great many trade-offs between reach, e.g. one-way mass communication versus richness in terms of personal communication. Now, high reach is no longer a barrier for interactivity. And lack of face-to-face contact does not prevent richness in communication and purchasing processes. We move in the direction of *economics of information*.

Market Leadership – Old Economic Rationales under Pressure?

Marketing is a management discipline meaning a set of values supporting certain company culture characteristics. Marketing is also a "technique" for decision-makers allocating resources to reach "optimal" – and therefore specific – goals under dynamic market and competitive conditions. Marketing deals with understanding, uncertainty, and application of business economic rationales. The questions "why", "where", "how", and "when" to allocate resources do not disappear in the future. However, there is more evidence that economic effectiveness and quality in customer relationships must be viewed as a separate strategic issue in marketing. Who says that market leadership *per se* means dominance, gorilla thinking and the highest market share? What happens when economies of scale are linked more to network economics than to accumulated experiences? In that case, agility and fast movers might eventually break the marketing codes of former market leaders. The thunder flies will win.

Consequently, the idea comes up that the attributes of exchanges, i.e. reciprocity, interdependence, partnership and transparency, vis-à-vis every single customer create more profit and value for the company than "negotiating power" and "market dominance" would. New ways to market leadership are becoming attractive.

Future Marketing Paradigm

A new, dynamic paradigm for marketing management rooted in relationships is gradually emerging and works its way to boardrooms, graduate teaching and consulting. It is nourished by an explosively increasing amount of research. It gets further stimulation from more and more of best practice cases, where a growing number of customers design their marketing strategies, organisational structures and business models along with a relationship perspective.

Traditional strategy and marketing textbooks treat customer-supplier relations as an add-on – an extra dimension within the existing theoretical frames of reference. The relationship perspective has been viewed as a modification of accepted marketing theories – a new parameter among others to count for.

What we need, though, is a new marketing paradigm *founded* on relationships and hence the dyadic perspective. Why? Well, because relationships are becoming the backbone of any competitive business and hence also the key to market success. Because competitors become our partners as well!

Objectives

When we began writing this book, we had a very clear objective in mind. We wanted to demonstrate that a relationship approach to marketing could and should be developed into a discipline of its own. In our view, this would require the design of a completely new relationship marketing framework. A framework resting on business economics and integrating the best of the existing marketing management thinking. A framework derived from basic and great theories of relationship behaviour and business strategy. A framework providing conceptual insights as well as inspiration and applicable techniques for strategic marketing purposes.

Research in relationship behaviour and relationship marketing has brought a lot of strong evidence supporting the claim that the relationship aspect plays a central role in the understanding of markets and company behaviour in real life. The research not only draws such conclusion from empirical evidence. Research has also delivered theoretical models of behaviour and marketing systems that can actually describe and explain relationship patterns and market structures.

Our objective is to structure, integrate and synthesise what we know about strategic relationship marketing across research boundaries in one framework of analysis and strategy formulation. Based on this framework, the reader should not only get a complete overview of the why's, what's and how's of strategic relationship marketing, but also a series of logic links between traditional marketing thinking and definitions on the one hand and relationship marketing models on the other.

Target Audience

As a textbook writer, one must be careful in the definition of the target audience. First of all, this book is not a handbook or check list like a "how-to-do-it" book. Secondly, we consciously aim at giving our reader a mental roadmap to dyad marketing in terms of definitions, models, archetypes, parametric overviews and analytical templates and methodologies.

Both authors have long-standing professional backgrounds within business life management and in academia. We are convinced that practitioners do seek frameworks for conceptual understanding and mental landscapes for decision-making, and that relationship marketing in particular is currently considered to be a crucial matter in most companies.

In summary, we therefore have graduate students, scholars, management consultants and marketing practitioners as our target audience. They all demand a new dyad marketing framework! Implicitly, some parts of the book, though, assume an insight in general marketing management and mainstream strategy models as well as basic business economic theories. Therefore we recommend our reader to first become acquainted with the basic principles of strategic marketing management!

We wish you a pleasant journey to the land of customer relationship marketing.

Acknowledgements

Writing a book does not come easy, despite the fact that it may look that way when the process is undertaken and the list of contents gradually emerges during the first phase.

Gradually, the process turns into a project and if managed as such, the result will actually be a complete work. However, this cannot be done without the support and understanding from the surroundings, sources of information, and interested case firms.

We would therefore specifically dedicate our acknowledgements to our families – particularly Marianne and Annette – and our colleagues who have commented on and discussed the ideas of this book.

1. The Relationship Aspect of Marketing

1.1 Introduction – the Power of Relationships

It is a common experience that the relationship between a customer and a supplier can be very strong and sometimes almost impossible for others to challenge.

In this opening chapter, we will introduce the basic framework for the understanding of relationships between buyers and sellers and what might eventually make relationships almost unbreakable. Recognizing the power of relationships as a key aspect of strategic marketing also means that the marketing concept for the future must be renewed and the marketing literature rewritten.

Consider the following situation: Two competing construction companies make a bid for a major, prestigious contract. One of the two companies has maintained a long, close relationship with the customer. The two competing firms' offers are almost identical in price, quality, delivery and service. Who do you think will win the game and get the account? Now, what do you think would happen, if the proposed budget presented by the supplier with the long-standing buyer relationship is 5% higher – with the quality and other terms still being identical? What if the price difference is 9%? Or even 24%?

The outcome depends on many variables. It depends on the cultural context of the relationship, the managerial policies within the buying organisation and a multitude of other factors. Generally, however, the buyer will always be influenced by the previous relationship experiences with the two competing suppliers.

As mentioned, there is conclusive evidence that the supplier-customer relationship is an essential part of what goes
on in business life and always has been – be it rational or
not. So, the relationship approach to marketing is genuine
and important. Relationship capital counts, and marketing
in a relationship perspective requires specific attention and
explanations not necessarily in accordance with the exchange-
centric perception of marketing So, the fact we build on can
be narrowed down to this fundamental assumption:

The value of relationships > The value of exchanges

The assumption makes it necessary to adjust the understanding of marketing as a discipline and of marketing management as a company philosophy. Hence, the existence of the
intrinsic value of relationships is also a strong stimulus for
researchers to establish a new paradigm of marketing strategies.

In relationship marketing management, the focus is on
the overall rapport between customer and supplier, not just
on the individual episodic exchange between them. Creating, building and preserving relationships becomes the real
value driver behind competitive advantage and outstanding
performance. In that respect, relationship marketing is the art
of initiating and maintaining profitable relationships, turning
prospects into customers and customers into friends.

Taking the above example from the construction industry
to the next level, it can thus be argued that there is a distinct
correlation between the long-term profitability of a company
and its customer relationships. Relationships must then be
considered an intangible asset – an external, not fully controlled resource base.

As shall be demonstrated later, outstanding customer relationships, longstanding consumer loyalty and competitive
advantage in the marketplace are not just results of generally satisfying customers. It takes much more than that. It
demands extremely satisfied customers. This highest rung on

the customer satisfaction ladder can, however, be difficult and risky to reach.

Systematic analysis of relationships as well as the economics of such relationships can help companies increase their marketing skills and improve their overall market performance. In fact, the customer with the building project might very well end up saving money by choosing the project with the highest proposed budget. Why? It is due to the fact that existing relationships often are combined with more effective regulating mechanisms, e.g. smooth cooperation, trust and partnership and hence they are less costly to administer. Therefore, a buyer must consider the cost of breaking the relationship, before deciding which supplier to use. Consequently, also marketing professionals must take the relationship aspects into consideration in their marketing strategies.

1.2 What Business is Marketing Really in?

It has been suggested that relationship marketing is no more than taking marketing back to its roots. Accordingly, it can be claimed that the relationship approach to marketing represents a kind of "backward" paradigm shift.[1] Throughout the history of modern marketing, the leading marketing management theories have focused almost entirely on fast moving consumer good industries. The main thrust of marketing strategies in the past was based on the belief that the optimal marketing approach was to know how, when and where to position your product to make consumers buy. The dilemma between the exchange-based and the relationship marketing concept can be summarized as shown in fig. 1-1.

These two definitions draw on distinctly different theoretical sources. The classical definition (left) underscores business success through careful planning made and executed by specialists under straight, centralized managerial control. This is the management regime definition.

The marketing mix in terms of product, price, place and promotion is what is going to convince the consumer and

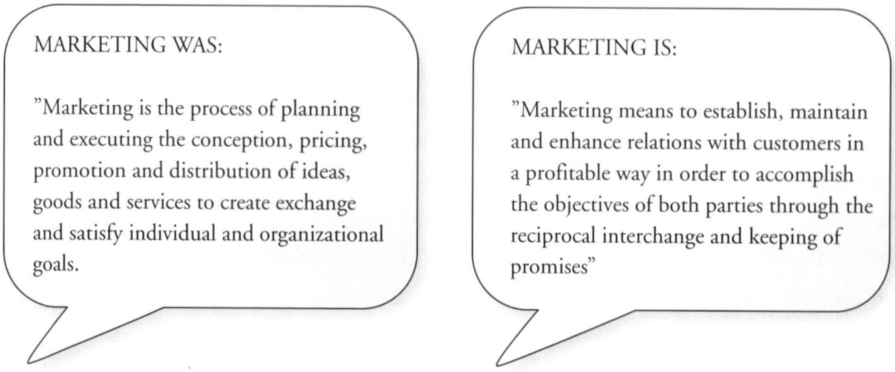

MARKETING WAS:

"Marketing is the process of planning and executing the conception, pricing, promotion and distribution of ideas, goods and services to create exchange and satisfy individual and organizational goals.

MARKETING IS:

"Marketing means to establish, maintain and enhance relations with customers in a profitable way in order to accomplish the objectives of both parties through the reciprocal interchange and keeping of promises"

Figure 1-1: What business is marketing really in? Source: American Marketing Association, AMA (1985), Grönroos (1990; 1992)

create market dominance. The consumer's only possible response is…. to buy or not to buy! Any business success formula should be derived from the marketing concept: "Satisfy the needs of the consumers better and/or at a lower cost than your competitors allowing you to make an above average profit. John Egan[2] has expressed this view as follows:

"Despite the obvious problems, little was changing in marketing education. Marketing theory remained mired in a futile search for laws, regularities and predictability. The marketing mix was (is) still the dominant marketing model, although it was seen as offering a too seductive sense of simplicity…. The toolbox approach of science-oriented marketing was criticised as a neglect of process in favour of structure leading to a consequent lack of study into other key variables….

So it appeared that marketing, the leading department of the first three-quarters of the century, was loosing its primacy…. Marketers were so busy attending to the practise of marketing that they may not have noticed that it was, for all practical purposes, dead. If not dead, it was certainly in crises."[3]

Excellent fast moving consumer goods companies like Procter and Gamble, Coca Cola, Lego or Disney would never have become so successful had their core competence not been within exchange-based 4 P marketing. But is that all?

The relationship-based approach to marketing – the definition (to the right) in figure 1-1 – does not deny the exchange as *the moment of truth*. But it relies on a different assumption. Marketing is about relationships: How they are established, develop, become consolidated and terminate. How they work, how expectations are created and promises kept. According to this approach, there will be many moments of truth. This definition recognises the voice of each individual customer. The marketing process does not stop after the purchase. In other words: "If the purchase is the courtesy, then the relationship is the marriage".[4]

A well-known CEO of a great company more than 70 years ago said it this way: "Your customers are your fortune".[5]

Even in traditional exchange-oriented business-to-consumer industries such as retail, insurance, financial services, IT, automobiles etc., it becomes increasingly clear that the heart of marketing lies in the relationship. Consumers have always been searching for positive relationships with suppliers and emotional associations to brands, because it makes buying easier. Not at any price, but within the range of tolerable cost differences. This, however, is nothing new.

What *is* new to marketing as a discipline is that it must revitalise itself by moving from "left to right" in the previous figure and redefine itself through a more holistic, consistent view of the customer.

1.3 The Classical Buyer-Seller Relationship

When is it reasonable to conclude that a relationship between two parties has evolved? The nice young person giving you a smile from the cash register in the supermarket? The local taxi company that your secretary calls whenever a cab is needed? The employment agency you used only once to hire

A SUPPLIER/CUSTOMER RELATIONSHIP IS:

"A relationship is composed of the sum of exchanges and contacts between supplier and customer over time combined with the regulating mechanisms that support and explain the parties* intensions for the future based on mutual understanding."

Figure 1-2: Definition of a relationship

an IT person with very specific skills? The accounting firm re-elected every year at the general meeting? When does a relationship become meaningful in this context?

One possible definition is presented in figure 1-2.
The level of understanding between the parties, the type of regulating mechanisms, the motives and the goals for future exchanges differ. In industrial markets, relationships are generally reciprocal or *one-to-one*. In consumer markets, it can to some extent seem artificial to use the term "relationship", as the supplier primarily communicates the 4 P one-way with the end customers – *one-to-many*. But that is also changing rapidly with information technology as enabler.

A company's portfolio of relationships is not only comprised of its customers, but of all its stakeholders such as suppliers, financial institutions, competitors, alliance partners etc. The exchange balance between inducements to and contributions from each stakeholder must still be kept competitive and dynamic in order to maintain the stakeholders' interest in doing business with the company. The relationship factor, however, may play an important role in the stakeholder "balances score"; and the relationship dimension may easily influence the relative balances as a consequence of intangibles such as trust and experience.

1.4 Elements of the Buyer-Seller Relationship

The simplified model in figure 1-3 illustrates the basic aspects of a relationship in a vertical supplier-customer structure. The exchange is the precondition for interaction which again is the precondition for integration.

When a company buys a commodity or a standard raw material with a transparent price structure in a perfect market, the procurement manager will typically act on a pure market basis. He will focus on the exchange. He will ask several suppliers for a bid and compare quality, price, delivery time etc. He will act within the constraints of an exchange-based con-

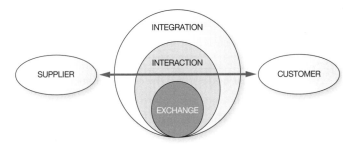

Figure 1-3: Elements of relationships between customer and supplier

tract framework. He may purchase through a dealer, broker or trader and has no particular interest in further interaction with the specific supplier. The supplier will ask for a payment guarantee. Pure market contracts are *exchange-centric*. The pure market contract leaves no or minimal room for trust and confidence.

At the opposite end of the spectrum, consider a car manufacturer working with a series of strategic subcontractor partners within a closely coordinated supply chain network based on just-in-time and joint R&D. The production plan for the upcoming week must be perfectly coordinated backwards within the supply chain taking into account the subcontractors and their supplies. In this case, the market mechanisms have been removed and do not function at the exchange level just described. The relationship is integrated into a semi-pyramidal, cooperative structure where the actors actively try to eliminate the friction between them. Therefore, network contracts are *integration-centric*.

In between we find thousands of different relationship hybrids. Many types of interactions require direct two-way communication between the supplier and the customer, often in the shape of mutual iterations in operational or strategic problem solving. This enhanced interaction between the parties develops over time and often at different organisational levels, either under managerial control or as bottom-up initiatives.

The *interactive-centric* relationships carry some elements of arms length control like in the pure exchange situations. But they are quite frequently inclined to also adopt integrative qualities.

A marketer must understand the characteristics and qualities of customer relationships before deciding on any strategic or tactical move. The structural attributes of relationships that are influencing the exchange, interaction and/or integration behaviour of the parties are composed of four distinctly different elements as shown in figure 1-4.

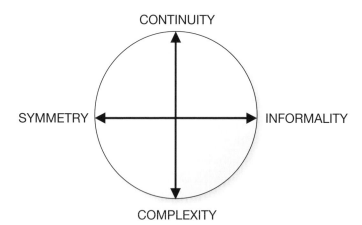

Figure 1-4: Structural attributes of relationships

Continuity means that the buyer and the seller have reached a stage of stability and repetition in their level and pattern of transaction. Rivalry still exists between the two parties and win-lose situations do happen during the ongoing trade between them. But both parties expect a mutual future, for which reason they seek consensus.

Many types of business relationships possess a high degree of embedded continuity. This is the case in most OEM product markets (original equipment manufacturing), where a company designs a component, a module or other features into an end product. In this situation, continuity is a result of product uniqueness and customer requirements. Another example of this is in the field of outsourced accounting or other business services. Accounting firms typically retain their clients for decades. This is due to the fact that all accounting firms have almost identical service packages governed by legislation and professional standards. Here, continuity is in fact rooted in non-uniqueness, which has created a "no-reason-to-change" market. In both cases the arguments behind continuity are relatively straightforward.

As shall be demonstrated later, continuity in customer relationships represents substantial value in terms of retention economics and is one of the key elements in all relationship marketing programmes and investments.

Relationships also differ in their degree of *complexity*. Relationships with high levels of complexity cannot only be difficult to manage, but difficult to break as well. This can lead to a breakdown in communication, redundancy, high control costs and simply mistakes in general. Complexity can be caused by:

- *The exchange*: High involvement durable goods and services such as buying a house or a new car means that very complex relationships between the individual and "the market" evolve. The same will be the case for companies seeking a sole distributor in a new market.

- *The interaction*: Social contact in the context of extensive networks of personal communication between people in organisations makes industrial relationships rather complex and difficult to change.

- *The integration*: Contracts and regulating mechanisms in business-to-business relationships can be complicated, incomplete and inconsistent. Very rarely does a contract cover all possible issues that can come up between two parties. Therefore they must rely on some kind of common problem-solving strategy or understanding. This can, however, also complicate the process.

Whereas continuity in relationships strengthens a business's ability to remain competitive, complexity can become a double-edged sword. Some companies follow a strategy that has a maximum level of complication in order to create an atmosphere of perceived dependence. In insurance and financial services, suppliers consciously try to deliver packages – bundles of products that are tied together in complex "all or nothing" relationship contracts.

A counter-strategy to this would be to reduce the level of complexity through unbundling – i.e. offering transparent, understandable ranges of products, where the customer can choose exactly what he or she wants.

Symmetry is the third structural characteristic of the buyer-seller relationship. Symmetry is a question of relative distribution of influence and information within the relationship. Asymmetry in a relationship can be a powerful motive for individuals as well as companies.

The superior party will tend to capitalise on the cost and effort which his counterpart will have to absorb in order to overcome the gap in knowledge or bargaining power. In some situations however, this approach would not be optimal. When the asymmetry is recognised by both parties, defensive measures such as lower quality, less knowledge sharing, and more control would be adopted be the weaker party.

Several studies[6] have demonstrated that a relationship between companies often continues despite the top management's decision to dissolve it. This is due to the *informality factor*. The real institutionalisation of a business relationship is created between people in organisations and not by command structures. People sometimes view employees in their counterpart organisation as colleagues and management as the enemy.

1.5 Classifying the Pattern of Interaction Between Buyer and Seller

Whereas the basic attributes of the traditional market relationship are external as well as within the company's control and used as part of a *marketing strategy*, it is also interesting to consider how effective a set of marketing actions will be in a dynamic perspective as a function of the customer's *purchasing strategy*. This can be illustrated in the following classification of supplier-customer relationships, see figure 1-5.

| | | Marketing Strategies | | |
		Competitive	Co-operative	Command
	Competitive	1 Independent	2 Mismatch	3 Independent
Purchasing Strategies	Co-operative	4 Mismatch	5 Interdependent	6 Dependent
	Command	7 Independent	8 Dependent	9 Mismatch

Figure 1-5: Generic classification of supplier-customer relationships. Source: Based on Sørensen (1997)

The relationship behaviour of a supplier in terms of exchange, interaction and integration can be based on any of the three marketing management philosophies:

- *Competitive:* A give and take, zero-sum attitude. What the customer gains, we loose. The regulating

mechanism will be based on arm's length and extensive control.

- *Co-operative*: Here, the assumption is that the customer will enter into a win-win relationship and will
work to the benefit of both parties. In this case, frictions are minimised and interdependence between
the parties will be the end result.
- *Command* relationship behaviour relies on opportunism and is based on pure dominance logic. The
philosophy is that a supplier can earn above normal
profits by making the customer dependent on the offering. The core of the relationship, i.e. the product,
is supposed to have unique qualities that influence
the customer to enter into a command relationship
in order to attain the product. The end result is the
dominant supplier and the dependent customer.

The generic purchasing strategies can be classified in the same
categories explaining the logic behind the behaviour of the
buyer as being either competitive, cooperative or command-
oriented.

Independent relationships are characterised by intense rivalry between supplier and customer. The relationship may have
a high degree of continuity and complexity. Independence
does not necessarily mean that there is a constant threat of the
relationship breaking down. But none of the parties are interested in testing the benefits of a closer cooperative structure.
Independence means that both parties consciously evaluate
alternatives and deliberately keep switching costs down.

A mismatch scenario occurs when a co-operative-oriented
supplier or purchaser is confronted with a counterpart who
has a competitive strategic approach. A co-operative style
seeks joint optimisation through the utilisation of the different capabilities in organisations. Mismatch occurs because
the competitive reaction is not commensurate with advantage of the invitation to co-operate. When suspicion is present regarding motives, control, lack of commitment, focus on

formal contractual arrangements etc. and even the potential for a win-lose situation is what meets a peacemaker, then the chances of reaching a positive result are minimal.

As shall be demonstrated later, *interdependence* assumes mutual trust and the inclination to optimise the relationship. This requires a co-operative marketing philosophy as well as a co-operative purchasing attitude. Both parties give up some of their autonomy, impose switching costs on themselves and assume the risk of trusting the other party. But even a mutually co-operative relationship needs regulating mechanisms in terms of control and outside pressure from competing relationships.

- In reality, only a few relationships are truly "generic" in the sense that a marketing strategy is solely based on e.g. a command relationship. Typically, it is a combination of different types of relationships and strategies. Furthermore, relationships are dynamic; they change over time and adapt to the actions of both parties and the mutual experiences.

In recent years, most companies have made radical changes in the structure and perception of their relationships to become an integral part of the implementation of new business models. There is a rapidly growing interest in relationship management as a key success factor, and huge IT investments have been made in order to organise, integrate and interpret relationship data. Value chains have become atomised and company roles become more focused on core competencies. At the same time, inter-company value chains have had to develop and become more integrated, which enables each company to remain competitive. In this combined focus-integration perspective, the relationship as such has become an even more important factor and hence also relationship strategies.

1.6 Defining Relationship Marketing

Kotler et al. have attempted to modify the traditional 4 P framework of marketing in a relationship-oriented direction. Kotler agrees to the notion that the marketing mix represents the *seller's view of marketing*. Hence, he and others suggest that marketers should view the 4 Ps from a *customer-oriented perspective* as demonstrated by the 4 Cs in figure 1-6.

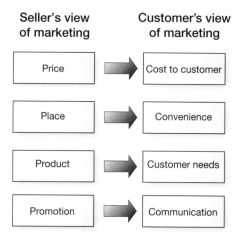

Figure 1-6: From 4 Ps to 4 Cs. Source: Kotler *et al.* (1999)

Every student is familiar with the 4 Ps. The 4 Cs, on the other hand, are new. The 4 Cs are an expression of what the 4 Ps mean to the customer. The P for price is a C for cost in the customer's mind.

This contribution is valuable for some marketers, but it does not represent a paradigm shift or a new relationship-based marketing definition. It is an attempt to update the marketing mix, but it stills sticks to the toolbox view of marketing as positioning. Although there are many aspects of marketing management, the relationship approach appears to have a substantial impact on long-term business success. We will define relationship marketing as in figure 1-7.

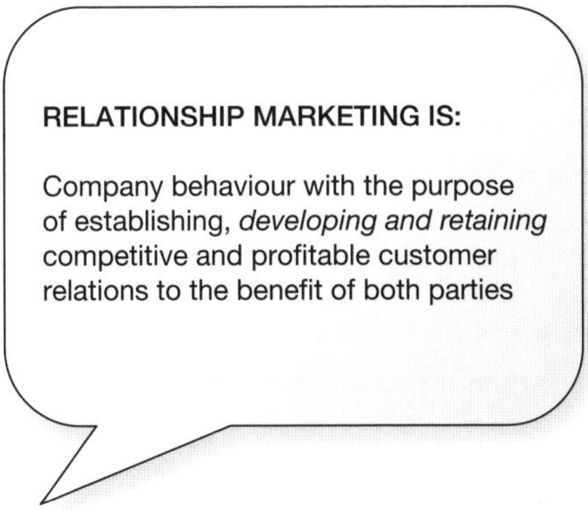

RELATIONSHIP MARKETING IS:

Company behaviour with the purpose of establishing, *developing and retaining* competitive and profitable customer relations to the benefit of both parties

Figure 1-7: From a seller to a customer perspective[7]

We do not consider marketing to be a strictly parametric, programme-oriented discipline, but *a pattern of total organisational behaviour*. Additionally, we consider interdependence, mutual co-operation and commitment between supplier and customer to be absolutely crucial aspects of relationship marketing.

This definition has no ethical basis. Neither does it reflect "good will" per se. The basic notion "for the benefit of both parties" introduces the idea of optimising relationships because it is the most profitable long-term strategy. No more – No less. The bottom line is still the bottom line. The relationship as a whole is considered to be the key to competitive advantage.

Relationship marketing principles do not exist in opposition to traditional segmentation/positioning marketing approach with regard to techniques and marketing mix decisions. Likewise, it would be a mistake to look at the relationship dimension as one tactical approach among others. Relationship marketing is a fundamental managerial approach to business. The basic belief is that reduction of frictions in networks of trade is a prime source of profitability.

The definition above also indicates that not all relationships are profitable. Relationships that are profitable on a lifetime basis may be loss-making in some stages during the life-time. The recognition of potential loss-making relationships suggests that marketing management must pay attention to three different objectives in terms of:

- The management of the initiation of customer relationships.
- The maintenance and enhancement of existing relationships.
- The handling of relationship termination.

Marketing management introduces two new aspects to the marketing process: *Customer deselection* and *management of different stages of the relationship*. Both elements play key roles in profitability.

1.7 Different Theoretical Directions in Relationship Marketing

Relationship marketing is a relatively new discipline still in search of common ground and well-accepted frameworks. Various sciences have contributed to the systematisation of marketing into a viable research and teaching discipline: Economics, psychology, sociology, political science, mathematics and many more. Relationship marketing as a discipline draws upon these sources as well.

Today, there is no commonly accepted theoretical foundation and no commonly accepted paradigm of relationship marketing. Different research approaches come into play here[8]. Their origins, the complexity of problems studied and their research methodologies differ widely. Some of the main approaches to relationship marketing are shown below.

The four main schools in relationship marketing do not represent an evolutionary process. They have developed independently of each other.

	POSITIONING STRATEGY APPROACH	TRANSACTION COST APPROACH	POLITICAL ECONOMY APPROACH	NETWORK INTERACTION APPROACH
CONTRIBUTORS	Borden, Kotler	Williamson	Arndt, Skytte	Hedaa, Grønroos, Gummesson
FOCUS	THE MARKETER	BUYING AND SELLING PARTIES	SYSTEMS OF EXCHANGES	COMPLEX SOCIAL PROCESSES
RELATIONSHIP VIEW	A TACTICAL TOOL TO BUILD CUSTOMER LOYALTY	A BALANCE OF ECONOMIC RISK/ RETURN CALCULATIONS	A MIX OF DYADIC FORCES	MUTUALLY INTER-DEPENDENT CLUSTERS
MARKETING SCOPE	SEGMENTATION/ POSITIONING	CONTRACTUAL DOMINANCE	SINGLE PARTNER PERSPECTIVE	TOTAL VALUE CHAIN
INTENT	NORMATIVE: PLANNING AND PLAN	NORMATIVE: ACTIVITY STRUCTURING	DESCRIPTIVE: ANALYTICAL FRAMEWORK	DESCRIPTIVE: SYSTEM BEHAVIOUR

Figure 1-8: Overview of main relationship marketing approaches

The *positioning strategy approach*, which in fact covers a rather heterogeneous body of literature, does not consider relationships to be the most important marketing dimension. Through the marketing mix (the 4 Ps), the intention of marketing is to position the offering of the company or the business unit vis-à-vis target groups identified and prioritised through careful market segmentation and competitor analyses. The relationship dimension is an "extra", a tactical, add-on resource allocation tool among many others that a marketer can use.

The transaction cost approach is a theoretical field that can be used within a relationship-marketing framework, but it was not developed as such. The thrust of this so-called institutional economics school is basically that the transactional system, i.e. the relationship, has a huge impact as a driver of costs and benefits. Markets, buying and selling strategies and the contractual terms under which supply and demand meet cannot be explained without understanding all potential obstacles, all the pros and cons and all the in-between arrangements between two parties. That is, the complex and challenging trade-offs between arm's length and deep partnership. Institutional thinking assumes a kind of Darwinist world order in which own-interests orientation is the key to understanding market behaviour. One of the main discussions under the institutional economic paradigm is activity structuring, i.e. the optimal composition of internal activities ("make") versus externalisation of activities ("buy"), and which marketing management challenges are arising from different activity structures.

The *political economy paradigm* discusses the comprehension and articulation of organisational behaviour and hence relationship marketing in more depth than institutional economics. This approach offers a holistic framework for analysing how and why exchanges take place, how two or more customer-supplier parties interact and relate. It outlines different profiles or archetypes of strategic behaviour, which can be used to create and execute single partner strategies; the ultimate relationship marketing solution.

A famous and genuine attempt to create a new relationship-oriented marketing paradigm is the IMP[9] group. Their starting-point was an amazing curiosity with regard to relationships and markets. For reasons of simplicity, all the descriptive, social-oriented approaches to relationship marketing are labelled the *network interaction approach*. This was not done with the intention of giving the marketer or the market analyst any specific methodologies or techniques to create substantial competitive advantages. But the network approach has indeed made a substantial contribution to the study of vertical supply chains. It has been able to explain how clusters of companies act and where obstacles and limitations may arise and why. It does not pretend to judge what is good or less good marketing, but it has inspired us to create more application-oriented models in particular on business-to-business markets.

In the following chapters, all four approaches to strategic relationship marketing will be drawn upon, not just the one of them. It is necessary to present all of them as they all work together to make a comprehensive set of relationship marketing rules and principles and therefore none of them should be excluded. Having said so, the main layers under the theories and models in relationship marketing, which we will introduce and discuss throughout the book, are *the economic and dyadic perspectives.* A dyad is a relationship between two parties and the relationship-oriented behaviour of the parties seeking balanced solutions in an environmental context. We believe that the economic forces and rationales behind human behaviour in business can best be understood if relationships are in focus and if one recognizes the idea of optimisation.

2. A Systematic Approach to the Buyer-Seller Relationships

2.1 Marketing as Mutual Exchange

That marketing should be regarded as exchanges in dyadic relationships, i.e. the two parties involved are regarded as a "closed" relationship without interference from outside, is not a recent observation.[10] However, it still seems to be new to many marketers that focus must be on the outcome for both parties – simultaneously. In addition to this, one of the most significant differences between relationship marketing and traditional marketing is that it is necessary to identify the needs and demands of the customer's customers in order to satisfy the customer's demands in an on-going perspective. This does not only require a clear understanding of the customers' demands, but also the customers' motivations to formulate their demands in the way they have. This is comparable to the change of focus when selling a product because of its features to focus on the customer's benefits from using the product.

On top of this, exchange may take place if there is perceived value by at least one of the parties. The important implication of this comment is that the relationship will benefit in total if at least one of the parties is better off. Regarding the relationship in the dyadic perspective thus provides a picture of the total outcome of the relationship, and not merely a "one-sided" picture. Therefore the focus is not merely on the individual party, but on both parties simultaneously and holistically. An example of this would be that if you could inform your airline operator of your travel needs in advance, they would be able to plan ahead and thereby optimise the necessary capacity and give you a lower price on the ticket.

We have to go back to Kotler[11] to find that the term "relationship marketing" was added to the definition of marketing as exchange. Kotler saw relationship marketing as the way in which suppliers try to:

> "… build up long-term, trusting, "win-win" relationships with customers, distributors, dealers and suppliers."

Kotler further argued that organisations would be able to lower the transaction costs as they build trust and develop an interest in cooperating with one another. It is important to note that the definition is still a "one-way" understanding of relationships, i.e. it is the initiating organisations that build relationships.

This is in line with the IMP-group[12] and their focus on relationship trust[13]. Another parallel is the introduction of the "marketing network" concept introduced by Kotler to further explain the concept of marketing:[14]

> "A marketing network consists of the company and the firms with which it has built a solid, dependable business relationship and thereby has built good relationships and profitable transactions will follow."

Thus, the marketing concept has gradually changed its focus towards processes and a more long-term perspective. However, relationships are still perceived as a result of activities managed by the initiating organisation, i.e. the "one-way" perspective. Strategic relationship marketing challenges this type of thinking, as it regards mutual exchange to be a basis for building mutual beneficial relationships.

The introduction of marketing systems has, however, altered this one-way perception considerably and this was where the introduction of the "two-way" marketing concept came into play.

2.2 Marketing as Systems

Exchange is the most basic[15] activity in marketing, but exchange needs to be linked to the parties responsible for the exchange and the variables affecting them.[16] Therefore exchange is described as part of a marketing system or exchange system:

> "In essence, the exchange system may be defined as a set of social actors, their relationships to each other, and the endogenous and exogenous variables[17] affecting the behaviour of the social actors in those relationships."

Examples of *endogenous* (internal as seen from the relationship's point of view) variables could be benefits from previous exchanges, evaluations of know-how and expertise of the other part, and expected benefits from future exchanges. The endogenous variables highlight the principle that all transactions must be regarded as part of a greater entity and that a transaction cannot be evaluated on its own.

Examples of *exogenous* (external as seen from the relationship's point of view) variables are competitive situations, competitive limitations and laws regulating the area of transaction. The central comment related to these variables is that the interplay between the endogenous and exogenous variables will determine the volume of the exchange.

The relationship must therefore be seen as a result of past experiences[18] combined with the expectation of positive interaction in the future. Furthermore, the importance of internal factors, as well as external factors, is stressed as they influence the exchange and the content of the exchange.

2.3 Three Types of Exchange

The system approach also presents three different forms of exchange,[19] based on the notion that marketing is about understanding why people and organisations engage in exchange relationships and how exchanges are created, resolved or avoided:

- Restricted Exchange
- Generalised Exchange
- Complex Exchange

Restricted exchange, or dyadic exchange, takes place between two parties, A and B, and only two (this is why it's called *restricted*). The relationship between A and B can be described as follows: A <-> B. These parties could be end-users, retailers, salesmen, manufacturers etc., and the "<->" symbolises that A and B simultaneously are supplying and receiving goods, money, information etc. The continuous existence of the dyad is based on mutually beneficial exchanges as seen from both parties' point of view where both parties contribute and benefit. In short, these are exchanges involving only two parties, and the exchanges flow in both directions.

Generalised exchange takes place between, at least, three parties, A, B, and C, or more. Generalised exchange, in principle, covers all *one-way exchanges* taking place between more than two parties, hence the label *generalised*. The relationship between A, B, and C can be described as follows: A -> B -> C -> A. The "->" symbolises that it is a one-way direct exchange. The exchange takes place directly between the parties, and an example could be the FMCG-sector with A as the supplier, B as the retailer and C as the end-user. In short, these exchanges involve more than two parties, but the exchange flow is only one way – in terms of for example food products that flow only one way.

Complex exchange takes place between at least three parties, A, B, and C, or more. In principle, complex exchange covers all two-way exchanges that take place between more than two parties and is therefore *complex*. The relationship between A, B, and C can be described as follows: A <-> B <-> C. The exchange is direct between A and B, or B and C – and indirect between A and C. A wholesaler is a good example of complex exchanges and would be (B), as the ability to transform the offer from the supplier (A) to the end customer (C) and vice versa. To summarise, these exchanges involve more than two parties and exchanges are flowing both ways.

The type of exchange will provide you with a description of the number of participants, whether the exchange is direct or indirect and whether exchanges are one-way or two-way. In other words, it is merely a way to describe the direction and complexity of the exchange in question.

However, one thing is to define the direction and complexity of exchange, but it is crucial to consider *what* is being exchanged. The content of exchange can be put into two basic categories.[20]

2.4 Two Approaches to Exchange

The first category, *Utilitarian Exchange,* is more or less based on the concept of "Economic Man" and rational behaviour, maximisation, complete information and no external influence. The utilitarian exchange is the exchange of goods and services and is widely described in distribution channel literature.[21] In the distribution channel literature, the seller develops relationships in order to handle exchanges with buyers who serve two purposes; they are buyers of the products and at the same time they are handling the distribution task for the seller.

The second group, *Symbolic Exchange,* is based on the psychological, social and other non-physical transformations between two or more parties. This form of exchange may be described as adding the perception of what a product or service means to an individual, and not just focusing on what the product or service can do. This form is based on the expectation of the exchange; one will participate in an exchange because it feels right. This approach to exchange is only mentioned indirectly in the literature; perhaps it belongs to the physiological and sociological sphere. It is, however, clearly used as a marketing tool, especially with regard to perception of status, culture or fitness and is therefore extremely relevant in this context.

Most exchanges cannot be identified as either or, but will often be characterized by elements from both approaches. Therefore, the two groups of exchange are combined in what is called *Mixed Exchange.*[22] Mixed exchange means that the exchange can be characterised by utilitarian and symbolic elements simultaneously. An overview is introduced in figure 2-1.

	Utilitarian	Symbolic	Mixed
Restricted	2 parties involved in exchanging both ways due to mutual benefits	2 parties involved in exchanging both ways because it feels right	2 parties involved in exchanging both ways because they expect benefits
	Hard- and Software	Love	Marriage
Generalised	More than 2 parties involved in one-way exchanges because of mutual benefits	More than 2 parties involved in one-way exchanges because it feels right	More than 2 parties involved in one-way exchanges because they expect benefit
	Assembly line		
Complex	More than 2 parties involved in exchanging both ways because of mutual benefits	More than 2 parties involved in exchanging both ways because it feels right	More than 2 parties involved in exchanging both ways because they expect benefit
	Auditing	Sponsoring	FMCG-sector

Figure 2-1: Combining types of exchange and approaches to exchange

Furthermore, relationships must be understood in terms of both *individual (personal)* and *institutional (organisational)* relationships. This distinction may also help the reader to recognise that the individual is often the vehicle around which organisational relationships are developed and maintained. Some of the original studies of relationships[23] were actually based on industries where standardised products were sold. They found that relationships were primarily between individuals, not between organisations.

Describing exchanges must include time, partly because *how* exchanges take place develop over time, and partly because *what* is exchanged may change over time. Time was introduced as an important dimension[24] influencing the relationship and the exchange processes. Time seems especially important when understanding the reasons and background for the development of relationships. Why is it that some relationships take off in one direction and other relationships tend to go in other directions? Why don't they develop in the same manner, at the same speed and in the same way? And why is it that some exchanges are close and intimate while others are distant and formal?

To answer this we have to introduce a framework to describe relationships, their content, and their environment in order to identify potential influencing factors. The answers to these questions lie in the Political Economy Paradigm.

2.5 The Political Economy Paradigm

This paradigm is built around two central issues, *politics* and *economics,* both *internally* and *externally.* This structure makes it possible to work with the concept of power, internally and externally, as well as the concept of economic structures, also internally and externally. Internally and externally encompasses different things, depending on the unit of analysis. The unit of analysis may be the relationship, the dyad or a number of dyadic relationships.

- The *internal politics* and the *internal economics* of the entity in question, typically based on the dyad,
- *Political relationship* to the environment and *economic relationship* to the environment of the entity placing the dyad in a context,
- *The environment* relating to factors beyond the immediate context.

The political economy paradigm regards marketing as the

execution of a series of transactions and exchange processes. Another way of looking at it is that the paradigm uses the concept of social systems as a way to understand interaction within the dyad and between the dyad and its environment. The paradigm will be presented further in the text.[25] This framework is useful for analysing organisations as social systems and covers a variety of areas:[26]

> "Political economy is fairly general, as the paradigm may be applied in theory construction in a wide range of marketing areas. It is integrative through offering a unifying framework by incorporating major economic and socio-political constructs in the comparative analysis of marketing relationships."

The conceptual framework of the paradigm encompasses internal structures and processes, connecting them with the variables characterising the environment. These variables are called relationship variables. This group of variables is the connection between the social unit and the environment. The groups of components in the political economy paradigm are illustrated in figure 2-2. The illustration can be interpreted as a "Pandora's Box" or an onion, where you can analyse one layer in the relationship, only to learn that you have more layers to analyse once you are done with the first one.

Relationships are based on the rational arguments and emotional symbolism as introduced in figure 2-1. In figure 2-2, it is taken a step further and argues that the analytical view of economy and power is useful for identifying and describing how a relationship is influenced by these variables. Furthermore, it must be emphasised that the relationship is part of the environment whether in close or distant proximity. The point being that relationships cannot be understood as isolated entities as they are part of a larger body and the relationships both affect and are affected by this body.

The basic idea behind this conceptual framework is that the unit of analysis (the inner box) is connected through re-

Environment	Relationships to the environment	Internal Structure and Processes
		Internal Politics
	Political Relationships	Goals of the social unit
		Distribution of power **Politics**
	Dependence relationships	Boundary-spanning positions
	Inter-organisational form	Mechanisms for managing conflicts
Characteristics of the environment	Control mechanisms	
Proximity		
Capacity		
Differentiation		
Concentration	Economic Relationships	Internal Economics
Turbulence		Structure of the social unit
	Competitive markets	Internal exchange processes
	Quasi-integrated systems	Incentive systems **Economics**
	Integrated vertical marketing systems	

Figure 2-2: Major component groups of the political economy paradigm. Source: Based on Skytte (1990, p. 33)

lationship variables (the middle box), which depends on the environment (the outer box). In other words, all relationships must be understood and analysed within a context. This context may be the immediate surroundings, the middle box, or the environment, the outer box. I.e. the relationship cannot be understood or analysed merely in relation to itself. We have to look at potential influencing factors in the political and economic sense.[27] Thus, we are combining the analysis of the relationship with analysis of the environment as a sphere in itself.

The boundaries and external variables of the unit of analysis will depend on how the analytical unit is chosen and defined and, of course, analysed later on. The analytical unit could be a network (e.g. the Nissan car dealers in UK), a distribution channel (e.g. the Internet), a market sector (e.g. the pig farmers in Holland), relationships within an organisation (could be between the sales and logistics department) or the classical dyad (e.g. the supplier and customer), etc.

When determining the most suitable variables to use when describing the external environment in relation to theory development, a compromise was reached between detailed raw data and aggregated abstraction.[28] The first one could be a list of various interest groups and the second could be a classification of the external environment according to various dimensions or forces. In the political economy framework, these two methods are combined.[29]

The five variables used in the paradigm to characterise the *environment* are: distance, capacity, differentiation, concentration, and turbulence.

The *distance* variable describes the distance between the unit of analysis and the number of levels between the unit and the organisation and other external factors influencing the social unit. The distance variable is divided into three levels:

- The first level is the primary organisational environment, which contains suppliers and customers directly related to the social unit of analysis.
- The second level is the secondary organisational environment, which contains suppliers' suppliers and customers' customers.
- The third level is the tertiary organisational environment or the macro environment.

This environmental framework entails national economic, political, and legislative elements and will influence the social unit indirectly via the primary and secondary organisational environment.

The second variable, *capacity*, is related to the social unit's potential of acquiring production factors and the question of whether or not there is sufficient demand for the output(s).

The third variable, *differentiation*, is related to the homogeneity or heterogeneity of organisations, individuals, and socio-political factors that influence the social unit and its potential of acquiring resources. This will directly influence the level of required information for decision-making.

Concentration, is the fourth variable and it is related to the degree of resource concentration (e.g. if it is high or low), i.e. whether resources are concentrated in a few organisations or individuals or dispersed to many organisations or individuals. This variable is also related to geographic concentration.

The fifth variable, *turbulence*, is related to the pace of change and the dependency between the change processes in the input and output markets of the social unit and other environmental factors. Turbulence is often caused by changes related to external forces or resources and is therefore difficult to identify for the social unit. Hence, it may be difficult to obtain sufficient information for planning purposes and decision-making.

Focusing on the concept of exchange highlights, the dyad is the central object. The dyadic approach is an important theoretical contribution to the understanding of relationship marketing, as the existing literature neglects the importance of the dyadic relationships between the supplier and the customer. Therefore, the dyadic focus provides a theoretical structure for describing the relationship between a supplier and a customer.

In order to illustrate the flexibility of the political economy framework, figure 2-3 lists a number of typical units of analysis. They have been labelled in accordance with the units included in the unit of analysis.

The important point in figure 2-3 is that the unit of analysis may vary depending on the need, in other words, relationships can be analysed no matter if it is a dyadic relationship, a triadic relationship or a system of relationships. Thus, figure 2-3 highlights the flexibility of the political economy paradigm, as all four examples may be defined as the unit of analysis.

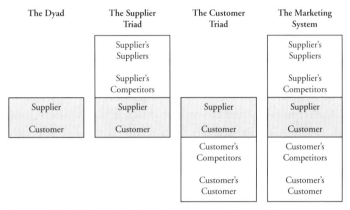

Figure 2-3: Different units of analysis in the political economy paradigm

3. The Economics of Customer Relationships

In the imaginary world of complete resource mobility, the relationship as a phenomenon is to some extent meaningless to discuss. Relationship considerations are not particularly important if the market is assumed to work entirely in a pure exchange-centric way independently of the context. If a supplier can replace a lost deal with a new one tomorrow at no extra cost, then a customer relation perspective is rather inferior.

If, on the other hand, a buyer and a seller doing business with each other on an ongoing basis eventually and gradually adjust to the needs, wants and structure of the other party in order to gain advantage, then the situation might be quite different. If a supplier even *adapts* his machinery, products, organisation, systems, staff or other capital assets in order to meet the *specific requirements* of individual customers or segments, such resources are no longer completely mobile. Assets adapted or even tailor-made to certain relationships, i.e. asset specificity, will presumably lose some, or maybe all their productivity, if the relationship breaks and the resources must find new, alternative "employment". This changes the economic rationales dramatically!

Traditional market economy axioms are rooted in the concept of a world without the kind of disturbances and irregularities that relationships tend to create and which tend to lead to relationships. So, the traditional pure exchange view is like a false mirror as it does not reflect what is going on in everyday business life. Relationships matter and therefore we have to express them in market-economic terms:

	The traditional marketing concept	The relationship marketing concept
Resource mobility	Complete – no asset specificity	Incomplete – asset specificity
Exchange friction	No friction between parties	Friction causing costs
Time frame dimension	Periodic short term view	Customer life cycle long term view

Figure 3-1: Principles of relationship marketing economics

Consider slogans like "the customer comes first" or "customers make pay-days possible" or "we try harder". These catch phrases are not just clichés, but are expressions that reflect the vision, values and corporate identity of a company. And they build on a customer relationship philosophy and not on a pure exchange perspective.

The Principle of Complete Resource Mobility

Complete mobility of resources means that a company can move its capacities and resources from one area of application or one type of customer to new purposes and other customers without any loss of return on such assets. The behaviour of the supplier and the customer is therefore not supposed to be influenced by resource mobility considerations such as a customer trying to unilaterally improve the bargaining power because of the supplier's specified assets or a supplier wishing to impose control over and create switching costs for its customers.

Additionally, it may be assumed that all companies have access to the same bundles of resources on the factor market, which then means that competitive advantages cannot be gained through unique resource combinations or core competencies.

The classic, well-accepted framework for marketing thinking maintains that sustainable competitive advantages are created by the capability of a company to exploit market opportunities better, cheaper, faster or more focused than its competitors, sometimes called the *s-c-p axiom* for structure (exploration), conduct (exploitation), and performance (execution).

The principle of market leadership based on a unique ability to build and defend long-term, mutually beneficial customer relationships more effectively than the competition represents the opposite view, i.e. that the resources and competencies generating the leading position on the market can neither be easily copied nor acquired on the factor market.

Relationship-based market leadership may impose a risk of dependence to the extent that the relationship competencies rely on customisation of assets to satisfy individual customer demands. Specified assets may be less valuable for other customers and hence such a trade structure requires particular protection measures via contractual mechanisms. The exchange view does not offer an explanation of this phenomenon.

Relationship economic thinking treats the economic value of an investment in customer specific assets up against the risks, which will inevitably follow. The classic marketing concept does not address this dilemma.

The Principle of Frictionless Transactions Between Supplier and Customer

In traditional business economics, it is assumed that the total, real price of a good or a service equals the sum of the costs consumed in production and distribution etc. This perception of total costs does not include the relational context of the production and procurement process. The traditional costing principle ignores that the *mere way of organising an activity,* i.e. producing versus buying, is in fact itself a key driver of costs.

Implicitly, this principle of frictionless transactions assumes that the only alternative to internal activity and hence the organisational hierarchy as the regulating mechanism between supplier and user is the *market exchange contract.* According to the idea of the classical market contract, a buyer can eliminate his or her risk, get the lowest price and obtain full transparency by an all-included contractual arrangement, such as a bill of lading in sea transportation.

But the real world is far from frictionless, when it comes to inter-firm activity. Where transactions are relationship-based, a completely new category of costs and benefits arises. The relationship is a *hybrid* kind of activity in between the perfect world of the classic external market contract and the smooth in-house production. The in-house production assumes mutual confidence between the transacting parties who are all members of the same organisation and under the same hierarchical umbrella. In hierarchies like corporate organisations, individuals are supposed to obey. Hence, the frictions are supposed to be at a minimum, although realities are often somewhat different from this ideal depending on factors such as reward mechanisms, corporate policies etc. Frictions are also supposed to be minimal using the market contract as regulating mechanism, but for the opposite reason, namely that the parties have agreed on a formal arrangement, by which they anticipate every possible situation and outcome.

Most economic activity does not live up to the *frictionless ideal* of either the intra-organisation exchange or the transparent market contract. The modified market mechanisms in the form of relationships introduce the costs of friction between two economic spheres. Managing the costs and benefits arising from those frictions between a buyer and a seller more efficiently than competitors then becomes a crucial strategic issue.

The Principle of the Period as Fiscal Dimension

For well-known reasons the period (year, quarter or month) is the key measurement interval in financial management and therefore also the vehicle in marketing management as well. The single time period can, however, only to some extent include the dynamics and the cause-effect mechanisms in market processes.

The Attention-Interest-Desire-Action effect hierarchy communications model (AIDA) is a good example. Costs of communication (creating attention) are paid in period x, whereas the outcome in terms of revenues (creating action) often materialises in period x++ (although difficult to measure with reasonable certainty).

Relationships between supplier and customer go through different stages over its lifetime. In this way, the most and maybe the only relevant economic approach to marketing from a relationship perspective is the principle of lifetime value of relationships and how it can be influenced by whom and when.

In recent years, interest in measuring relationship value has increased. One study concluded e.g. that every new pizza customer on average represented an amazingly high net present value of USD 5,000.

The lifetime perspective is not a revolutionary discovery. Most business people would agree to the economic importance of relationship elasticities such as volume, price, churn and duration. What people must find perplexing is that there is a desperate need for reliable theories and measurement tools in this area.

In the following sections, an overview of the core principles in the business economics of customer relationships will be presented.

3.2 The Business Economics of Customer Relationships – Risk and Opportunism

Research has demonstrated that the mere planning, execution and monitoring of customer transactions per se drives 25% of all costs in an average company – the price of "running the economic system".[30] Furthermore, several case studies have found a significant positive correlation between the durability of customer relationships and profitability. One study[31] e.g. concluded that a company, depending on the industry, could potentially increase the net present value of a customer relationship by 35-95% if reducing the churn rate by 5%. Although other studies have reached the opposite conclusion that old customers (business to business) tend to be less than average profitable, there is no doubt that the relationship dimension plays an important role as economic driver in the customer as well at the supplier organisation.

The phrase saying that it "costs ten times less to sell more to existing customers than to sell the same amount to new customers" is true in most situations, revealing the *acquisition economics* versus the *retention economics* dichotomy.

The following real-life story illustrates the importance of customer relationship economics.

Skanska and Rockwool[32]

Skanska is an international construction company with offices worldwide and a strong position in Sweden. Skanska is managed according to decentralised principles. Therefore, local managers, including the purchasing managers, make all day-to-day decisions.

Rockwool produces insulation materials of mineral wool and Skanska is one of Rockwool's biggest and most important customers.

Both Skanska and Rockwool operate on extremely competitive markets characterised by low margins and constant price pressure, where even minor deviations, delays or miscalculations can eliminate all profits from a given project. Some years ago, Skanska and Rockwool entered into a cooperative contract with each other with the explicit purpose of optimising the economics of the trade between them. In other words, Skanska and Rockwool aimed at replacing traditional exchange-centric thinking with relationship market economics.

The managerial motives for a switch from exchange to relationship terms of trade are illustrated in figure 3-2.

Before the relationship-based contracting was established, Skanska handled the purchase of insulation materials from project to project, most often in bid rounds where the suppliers of insulation, being a quite homogenous commodity, were played out against each other.

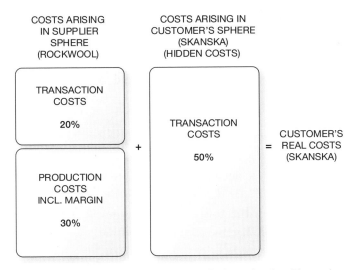

Figure 3-2: Skanska and Rockwool in the before-situation: The real costs of mineral wool at the arrival to the site. Source: Heikkila (1996)

This behaviour led to the astonishing cost structure shown in figure 3-2 above, which the parties to their surprise discovered, when they mutually decided to open their books in a joint analysis. The total costs arising in the supplier's, i.e. Rockwool's sphere, amounted to no more than 50% of the total price, Skanska actually paid. Series of hidden costs, such as inventory costs, loading and unloading, transportation, waste, loss, theft, delays of deliveries, broken deal costs and administration should be added to get a true picture of the business economic price.

The core production and administration expenses amounted to less than 25% of the total costs. The driver behind the remaining expenses was the frictions caused by the exchange-centric terms of trade.

In the pre-relationship situation, both parties pursued a *monadic*, sub-optimising objective, making use of the classical market contract. The monadic motivation is the opposite of the dyadic joint-optimising approach as introduced in Chapter 1.

The outcome was opposite from the intention of both parties, i.e. a dramatic rise in the price of insulation materials for the seller as well as for the buyer in terms of extremely high transaction costs, a subtle kind of "prisoners' game" where both opponents play a win-lose game and end up with a lose-lose result.

The True Product Costs

Even when a supplier and a customer develop an interdependent relationship based on cooperation, the rivalry within the relationship will not disappear altogether. Conflicts of interest are embedded in any buyer-seller relationship despite the strategic match, because each party wants the biggest slice of the pie. Therefore, the probability of conflict arises in any case. But it is not necessarily a zero-sum game!

The Skanska-Rockwool case shows the true costs of a sales or purchase exchange in business economic terms and not from an accounting angle, which is:

$$total\ costs = product\ price + transaction\ costs$$

In hindsight, it appears to be sound business logic for Rockwool to promote a relationship-economic, co-operative marketing approach, as the end result happened to be a win-win situation. Although it seems obvious and in the interest of both parties to mutually drive down the exorbitant friction costs stemming from *idiosyncratic behaviour,* where you are very conscious not to let your opponent become too influential, buyers and sellers rarely agree to just "open the books" with the idea of chasing joint optimisation and deepening the relationship. Instead, management most often prefers to stick to a pure or slightly modified market contract, as this regulating mechanism is considered to offer a maximum safeguard of self-interest, transparency and bargaining position.

As soon as the market contract is replaced by the hybrid relational contract, elements of risk and insecurity arise. The relationship contract contains a consciously chosen risk element, where the parties agree on a certain level of manoeuvrability and where confidence plays a key role as well. Risk is the cost, whereas saved transaction costs are the benefit.

Risk is revealed via *opportunism*, which is the flip side of the coin in any relationship. Opportunism means that a party, buyer or seller, will exploit and manipulate a situation to gain unilateral benefits at the expense of the counterpart. Opportunism can even stretch into what can be called "legal theft" in many bargaining processes.

The opportunity of developing "mutual benefits", which is an integral part of our relationship marketing definition, does not rest on idealism, but on a mere business self-interest calculation. What are the pros and cons of relationship contracts, balancing the benefits against the risks of the counterpart or perhaps one's own opportunism? Additionally, no decision-maker is completely rational or in possession of all information regarding alternatives and consequences.

Two kinds of risk are at play in any relationship. *Out-there risk* is caused by disturbances externally of the relationship, whereas opportunism in the relationship or expected opportunism leads to *in-here risk*. The opportunism and insecurity embedded in any relationship create idiosyncrasy and hence increase the costs, because they stimulate protection mechanisms. Ultimately, these protection mechanisms threaten the competitiveness of the relationship. So, for either party there is also the ongoing trade-off between the cost of risk and the cost of insurance through safeguard mechanisms.

The dyadic motive as opposed to the monadic motive, as touched upon previously, means that the buyer and the seller make systematic attempts to optimise the relationship by taking the interests of the other party into consideration as a matter of self-interest. The basic concept behind the dyadic approach is that a marketer should plan and execute such actions that minimise the customer's total costs, including the savings following managed frictional reductions. As demonstrated, this is not only a pricing issue. The contractual form of the relationship and the governing principles are equally important. Dyadic marketing concentrates on the overall relationship-economic cost-benefit balance within a competitive perspective. The ability to understand the game and the way cards are distributed in that game enables a player to define the best possible strategy for himself.

The *triadic* situation[33] includes the threats and opportunities stemming from the present or the potential relationships between a company's customers and its competitors.[34]

Risk and opportunism are guidelines for understanding and navigating through the mechanisms that are the basic concepts behind relationship marketing. The key economic expression is the transaction costs arising from the relationship parameters.

3.3 Customisation of Assets, Frictions and the Life Cycle

As mentioned earlier, customised assets or asset specificity[35] refer to the situation where an asset represents a lower economic value for a company in alternative employments than for the actual customer(s). Assets, which have been adapted to only one individual customer or application, have a positive impact on the relationship economy in that specific customer relationship. Customisation must be dealt with as a focal point and a crucial parameter in relationship strategies. Customisation of assets in that respect is in contrast to the idea of complete resource mobility in traditional business economics.

Customisation of Assets
Asset customisation can ultimately bring a supplier and his or her customer closer together. Consider the manufacturing company that invests in dozens of manufacturing plants, all working as subcontractors for only one customer. This is often the situation in relation to consumer goods, where leading firms like Coca-Cola, McDonalds and Marks & Spencer create a one-to-one sole supplier relationship with value subcontractors or partners.

The same level of *symbiotic relationships* can also be found in the relationship between airlines and handling agents and airline caterers or between newspapers and printing houses and in many other situations.

Dedicated, customised resources contribute to rationalise, protect and cost reduce the buyer-seller interaction; they create profitability for both sides and impose entry barriers for competitors and substitutes. Imagine what would happen if McDonalds decided to buy potatoes on the spot market every morning instead of contracting with manufacturers processing the potatoes on a long term basis. Any manufacturer that would offer an attractive price to McDonalds for a short-term deal would hardly succeed in breaking into the existing relationships.

Asset specificity can be a powerful marketing tool, but it also induces a high risk and an incentive to opportunism. Large companies very often have one sole or preferred supplier plus a second source. The idea is that the second source absorbs above peak capacity situations at the prime source, while at the same time safeguarding the customer company against supplier opportunism or bankruptcy. If assets like equipment, staff, sites or intellectual property rights are tailor-made to this specific important customer, the supplier is potentially vulnerable if the customer has a nearby alternative solution available.

Not all products or services that are perceived as customised within a certain range of features are individualised. *Mass customisation* does not imply the same level of risk and opportunism as previously described. Restaurants prepare the meal according to the taste of the guest without customising any asset. Car manufactures do the same when the customers choose an individual mix of design, colour and accessories.

Cost of Frictions

The Skanska-Rockwool example above illustrates how buying behaviour based on a market contract paradigm can lead to frictions in the physical and in the administrative system and hence also becomes generator of considerable and unnecessary costs. Frictions are derived from idiosyncratic reactions. The rational buyer assumes that optimal buying behaviour means using the market for each exchange, because any special preference for a supplier will be exploited by that supplier. Competitive pressure is what presumably prevents a supplier from excess pricing and term-twisting. Therefore, both parties must live with the frictional costs. The costs of idiosyncrasy are expected to be more than offset by lower prices. Markets are expected to be perfect or at least close to perfect.

In business-to-business relationships, it has become quite usual to distinguish between the *phase of negotiation* and the *phase of delivery*. During the purchasing phase, the market mechanisms are active. Existing relationship contracts are being stalled. Both parties act, and react, idiosyncratically; they distrust the motives, statements and calculations of counterparts. When an agreement has been reached, the parties enter into the phase of implementation. Both the seller and the buyer have an interest in minimising the frictions in processes like order flow, documentation, quality control, exchange of information and corrective actions if requested by the other party. The relationship is an in-between, hybrid, regulating structure and in many respects more complex to manage than the market contract or the hierarchy. Competition forces companies to concentrate on core skills only. This has created a demand for new management qualities, because the patterns of relationships change and become much more important. Whereas the idea of identifying and nursing a company's core competencies has become strategic mantra, the business economic discipline derived from that, i.e. to establish and administer customer and supplier relationships with a minimum of frictional costs, then becomes the key to competitive advantage.

Customer Life Cycle
The product life cycle and its underlying diffusion of innovation curve is the ancestor of most conventional marketing

strategy models from the BCG[36] matrix to Porterian thinking and crossing the chasm fascination. The composition of
a company's marketing programmes, in the form of the 4 Ps,
changes over the product life cycle because of market segments' attractiveness and competition.

All products, product categories and industries tend to
follow the bell formed development curve from birth to
death. The same pattern can be observed for customer relationships as well. In that respect, the customer life cycle or
CLC becomes the framework for the formulation of marketing programme prescriptions and of understanding the business economics of relationships from a lifetime perspective.
In contrast to the period as the time interval in programme
formulation and in impact measurement, the CLC relies on
a much more dynamic, cause-effect and customer-oriented
view of economics and marketing management. One possible
representation of the CLC concept is shown in figure 3-3.[37]

A customer relationship goes through different stages from
its emergence to late stage struggling and final dissolution. In
between, the relationship will develop as a consequence of the
rational behaviour of both supplier and customer. At the ma-

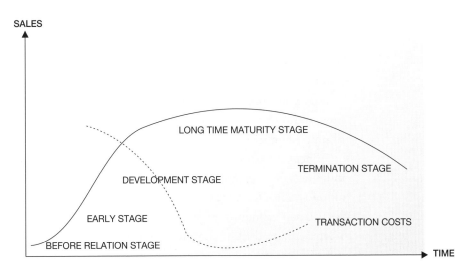

Figure 3-3: The customer life cycle

turity stage, the first signs of fatigue and restriction become apparent. Of course, points of disruption and cut-off will arise during the lifetime. Many customers e.g. simply reject to "marry" and break out in the meeting with the relationship chasm as a matter of policy.

In figure 3-3, we also illustrate how the transaction costs develop over the CLC. Initially, the idiosyncrasy, then trust and mutual adaption-driven cost reduction to final increase when unilateral incentives may eventually become the stronger ones.

The customer life cycle indicates the existence of four different concepts in relationship economics:

- Acquisition economics at the pre-relationship stage.
- Penetration economics at the early and the development stage.
- Retention economics at the long-term-/maturity stage.
- Termination economics at the end of the customer life cycle.

The economic calculations and the marketing tasks differ across the generic stages of the customer life cycle. At the pre-relationship stage, a company must invest time and effort to convince the customer to make a trial purchase, change supplier, take in a second source or buy a project. The costs of lost deals must be included as well. At the stage of acquisition, canvass sales, promotion, low margin orders, pilot installations and broken deal costs dominate. The headline is acquisition economics.

When a relationship has been established, the supplier mill move on to gain momentum with the customer in terms of time frame contracts, cross selling, share of pocket etc. The penetration-economic stages involve staff costs, solution development, product modification, but not rarely direct financial cash contributions to the customer organisation e.g. to buy shelf space and attention.

At the maturity stage, which may vary from weeks to decades depending on the situation, retention-economic considerations may be about prices and margins, costs of keeping competitors' entry barriers high, further product development etc.

Dissoluting a relationship can be rather expensive. Claims occur. Escrows and guarantees must be either cancelled or distributed. Some assets and employees may become idle which may result in new, partly unanticipated expenses.

It is reasonable to believe that the margin of profitability will increase (most apparent in business-to-consumer relationships) and that transaction costs will decline over the customer life cycle as a function of time, experience, confidence and possibly adaptation of assets. Some of the main factors supporting the idea of increasing returns over the customer life cycle can be summarised in a few headlines:

- High transaction costs at the beginning of the life cycle ("bargaining/pre-relationship") where monadic motives still dominate.
- Anticipation of opportunism and high costs of control as the market mechanisms still regulate the trade between seller and buyer. Hence prices are also lower.
- Higher costs of service, administration and mistakes at the earlier stages.
- Add-on revenues in terms of cross-selling, increase in volume and product line extension assume mutual confidence.

The customer relationship-profitability curve reflects a similar path.

A company may get stuck if, for some reason, the customer breaks off the relationship before or just after the CLC breakeven point. Retention economics in terms of prolongation of the life cycle and other kinds of add-on revenue streams then

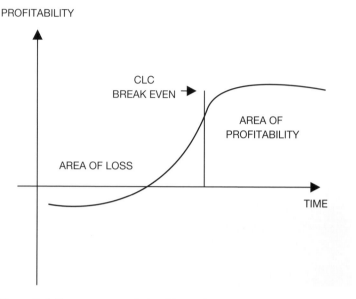

Figure 3-4: The customer relationship-profitability curve

become a key factor to understanding and improving overall performance.

Customer life cycle and relationship-economic coherence varies across industries. Some industries have extremely high entrance costs to relationships in terms of customised assets. This is the case with shipbuilding, heavy construction and in great many subcontractor industries, e.g. components to aircraft manufacturers etc. Often the CLC break-even point will be passed at a relatively late stage and profitability depends entirely on the marketing efficiency of the customer, e.g. the number of aircrafts of a given type being sold over the lifetime of the specific model. The same will be the case in industries with high customer acquisition costs such as in banking, insurance or asset management, where suppliers must invest in order to gain customer trust.

In other industries, which are also characterised by made-to-order and asset customisation, there will be no or at least very low expectations of continuity and life cycle. The marketing strategy must therefore be exchange-oriented and deliver profitability on the first order and on every order after this. In industries such as home construction, travel or some segments of consulting this will be the case.

Although relationship marketing focuses on acquisition as well as development and retention strategies, the element of retention value is often given more prominence. Indeed, it has become one of the underlying assumptions of relationship marketing that it encourages *retention economic rationales* first and *acquisition marketing* second. This bias exists because the relationship aspect is considered to be particularly beneficial on mature markets, which constitutes a vast majority of marketing situations. Also, the industries chosen most frequently as examples of successful application of customer retention strategies appear to have high front-end costs (selling costs) embedded in their business system.

3.4 Generic Transaction Costs

Customised assets, frictions and the "law" of the customer life cycle in the physical business system altogether are the drivers of transaction costs in the economic system. Perceptions of risk and opportunism determine how far two parties are willing to go in order to reduce frictions and develop a relationship that is based on interdependence. Relationship marketing develops competitive advantage by creating relationship-economic value and by inducing transaction benefits. Whereas the four economic concepts just described are built into the stages of the customer life cycle, so to speak, we must also pay attention to some basic generic types of transaction costs – not being attached to a specific lifetime situation.

The transaction cost basket is composed of the amount of money the buyer and the seller must pay in addition to the cost of the core service in order to execute the deal as illustrated in the Rockwool-Skanska case. There are three different types of transaction costs: Pre-exchange costs arising during the information-gathering stage, arrangement costs arising during negotiation and decision and post-exchange costs in terms of implementation and monitoring expenses. These are the *3 Cs of transaction costs: Contact, Contract and Control costs.* In principle, any exchange carried out by two parties at any of the life cycle stages imply a certain amount and mix of transaction costs.

How the underlying mechanisms in a *physical system* are the drivers of transaction costs in the *economic system* is summarised in figure 3-5.

	Contact Costs	Contract Costs	Control Costs
Acquisition economic stage	High	High	High
Penetration economic stage	High	High	Medium
Retention economic stage	Low	Low	Medium
Termination economic stage	High	Medium	High

Figure 3-5: Transaction costs across the economic life cycle stages

The qualitative transaction cost levels indicated in fig. 3-5 are approximations of an "average" CLS and are in accordance with the cost curve in fig. 3-3. Of course, the reality of business life is not that simple.

4. Customer Loyalty and Business Economics

4.1 Defining and Describing Customer Loyalty

The quest for loyalty has always been a cornerstone in human activity in general and in organisational life in particular. In a hierarchical power structure, members of an organisation accept the need of obeying leaders and following instructions. In ancient times, participants even swore their loyalty as an entry ceremony. In modern organisations, loyalty is also implicitly assumed and the reward-punishment system has loyalty as a central decisive factor. In hierarchies, market forces are eliminated. As long as you are a member of this organisational hierarchy, you must stick to our rules.

One thing is hierarchy – another thing is markets. Customers do not behave like organisational members. Loyalty is something a company strives to attain, not something that can just be requested or assumed. It must be earned. This is the case whether you work in a business-to-business context or you pitch for a relationship anchored brand loyalty on consumer markets. In both situations, you must give at least the same or even more than you receive – as perceived by your customer.

Customer loyalty conceptually implies both an *attitude -"think and feel"- dimension* and a *behavioural "do and experience"-dimension.* Neither one acts exclusively of the other. A few of the many definitions of loyalty highlights this assertion:

"Customer loyalty is the seller's perception of the con-

sumer's positive attitude to the product manifested by
rebuying".[38]

"The loyalty creating company is a company where the
entire organisation carries out conscious, ongoing and
effective efforts with the purpose of securing an optimal development of satisfied, loyal and hence profitable customers".[39]

We will work with the distinction between instrumental and
motivational loyalty. *Instrumental loyalty* is the kind of loyalty
most often found in business-to-business relationships. It is
related to the objective features and the functional dimensions of the product or service vis-à-vis a usage situation. *Motivational loyalty* is the predisposition emerging from a more
affective pattern of reaction, typically expected in consumer
markets. The rationale/cognitive and the affect-driven/emo-
tional reasons for loyalty are not per se contradictions and
are often mixed.[40] In both cases, the supplier must deliver
perceived relationship value in excess of the money the customers are paying.

There are many ways of classifying loyal versus non-loyal
customer behaviour. One such classification proposes three
ways of considering customer buying behaviour:

- *Switching behaviour*: where purchasing is seen as an
  either/or decision – either the customer stays with
  you (loyalty) or turns against you (switching).
- *Promiscuous behaviour*: Also an either/or situation in
  the sense that either the customer is loyal to you or
  flirts with many and various alternatives (promiscuous).
- *Polygamous behaviour*: Again, the customer makes
  a stream of purchases, but their loyalty is divided
  among a number of products. They may be more
  or less loyal to your brand or solution than to any
  other.

Consumer research tends to support the view that most cus-tomers[41] are in fact multibrand buyers and that only one out of ten consumers is 100% loyal. Consumers are constantly searching for products and services matching their specific needs. There is also doubt about whether loyal customers are more profitable than promiscuous and polygamous custom-ers are. Loyalists are often more light users, whereas multi-brand buyers are more heavy users within a specific product category.

4.2 The Customer Life Cycle and Various Loyalty Dynamics

The shape of the customer life cycle is a clear indication of the level and the sources of customer loyalty. There are several of such variations as illustrated in figure 4-1.

Customer relationships that *stabilise at the long-term stage* will typically be dyadic in their structure and mutually benefi-cial to both parties. The dyadic balance will come from cust-

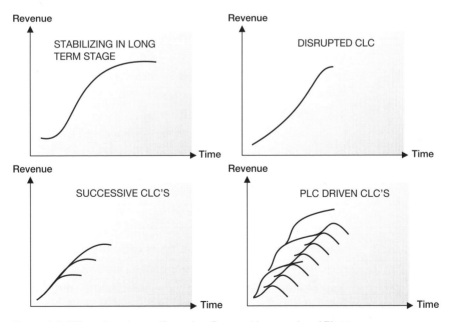

Figure 4-1: Different customer life cycles. Source: Hougaard and Bjerre

omised assets, co-operative relationship style, communication proximity of the parties, security, mutual commitment and probably also strong contractual agreements.

Almost all relationships are exposed to opposing pressure: Partly in the direction of deeper involvement, adaptation, cooperation and repurchase and partly in the direction of increased control, threat and dissolution to neutralise dependency and dampen idiosyncrasy.

In this battlefield of contrast forces, astonishingly many relationships do manage to stabilise and go on for a very long time. The co-operative forces tend to defeat the competitive destructive drivers.

Some relationships are *cut off suddenly and abruptly,* illustrated by the disrupted CLC. Some customers decide to break the relationship before the "relationship chasm" and reject the idea of moving into long-term stability. The reasons for this are many.

In knowledge-intense industries there is e.g. a high risk of relationship divorce, if a supplier begins to cooperate with the customer's competitors. Another situation is trade arrangements where the supplier is encouraged or even requested to invest in highly specialised customized assets, he will idiosyncratically evaluate the pros and cons of cutting off a customer relationship at the early stages (before investing) if there is a widespread belief that the customer is prepared to take unilateral advantage of the situation.

In relationships with *several successive mini CLCs,* the parties ride on the wave of good mutual experiences and inspiration. This will often be the case in project-oriented industries, where each project is a CLC in itself. The customer either tends to have preferences for the supplier in the next bid round or the supplier will bring new competencies and vitality into the relationship thus maintaining its competitiveness.

Customer loyalty should not only be viewed as a relationship-economic phenomenon. In some instances, the CLC is driven by frequent product innovations or renewals. We then talk about *product life cycle (PLC) driven CLCs.* In the software industry, new product generations appear regularly. The same is the case in the automotive industry. Whether driven by technology, fashion or other factors, the competitiveness of the core product or service is always a precondition for loyalty.

In some industries, we can distinguish between *always-a-share-customers* and *lost-for-good-customers* each reflecting very different CLCs. In the retail sector, consumers make use of most of the supermarket chains within their geographical reach. Depending on the buying motivation and situation, special offers or products etc., the consumer will choose to-day's shopping centre. It is interesting also to observe that the supermarket chains do no not primarily attempt to invest in customer loyalty through a more focused or differentiated chain profile. Location and category (e.g. discount) are apparently the most important features. This is a typical always-a-share market.

Lost-for-good customers are most often found in relationships with a high level of loyalty driven by confidence. If your doctor prescribes the wrong medicine or less dramatically, if your supplier of R&D consulting services becomes engaged with one of your major competitors, the relationship will often be terminated.

4.3 The Value of Customer Loyalty

Customer loyalty as a concept creates a strange paradox. Almost anyone will agree that true customer loyalty is a substantial intangible asset for a company – for branded products the most valuable asset of all – because it is the ultimate indicator of future sales and profits. Despite that, there are virtually no companies that have any factual-based knowledge about their customer's loyalty and the value of such loyalty.

It is necessary to decompose the value of customer loyalty into a number of value categories that can be analysed collectively and separately. We have developed the following typology regarding loyalty economy concepts:

- Lifetime economy – the ability of retaining the customer for a longer period of time.
- Efficiency economy – the ability to create dyadic cost advantages for the benefit of both parties throughout the CLC.
- Value adding economy – customer participation in the supplier's value generation.

In many cases, all the effects are active at the same time, but they do not necessarily pull in the same direction and it requires careful analysis to separate, measure and evaluate each of the loyalty value drivers.

Lifetime Economy

A loyal Cadillac customer once was said to be worth $ 332.000 over his or her lifetime[42]!

In a great many industries, profitability is heavily dependant on the lifespan of customer relationships, as already discussed. This is especially the case when the contact or contract costs are high compared to the rate of contribution per exchange or if investments in customised assets are substantial or if the experience cost effects are extraordinary. In such cases, the relationship contribution is negative until rather late in the CLC. Churn becomes a crucial economic driver.

On markets where lifetime economy is a critical factor, marketing must concentrate on giving the customers continuous motivations and arguments for them to keep coming back to do business. This will typically consist of positive inducements which confirm the value of the relationship for the customer stimulating repeat business e.g. annual bonuses or progressive discounts. A subtle way is to establish exit barriers through fees or non-refundable prepayments, administrative complications or systemic integration. Some industries have refined their exit barrier tool box to a high and petty subtle level!

The value of lifetime economics consists of three distinctly different elements:

Basic profits over a longer time span obviously increase the net present value of the customer relationship. In industries like IT, support and service contracts are common and in markets where revenues depend on subscription, licenses, spare part sales etc., increasing lifetime is an essential marketing task.

Add-on sales based on confidence. At the maturity stage of the relationship, the customer often tends to trust the supplier and will be positively inclined to cross-selling initiatives. When commercial banks began selling insurance or when Amazon.com extended the product line from books to a much broader range of consumer goods, it was clearly a way of capitalising on customer trust and other relationship ties.

Price premium. Loyal customers to a certain extent have decided to neglect the market forces with the purpose of harvesting on the advantages of low transaction costs. Loyal customers trusting the supplier will hence not pay attention to price increases; they might eventually become price inelastic. Loyal customers become the cash cow in many (consumer) markets. If, however, the greed of the supplier becomes too apparent – much like monopoly arrogance – customers may react extremely negatively.

Loyalty schemes have become widespread and popular as retainer tools. What some loyalty pioneers such as American Airlines and Tesco have experienced, is that loyalty programmes were effective and gave additional business in the beginning. But the incentive schemes rapidly became industry standard, which customers would expect from any supplier. All too quickly, early benefits were turned into unavoidable extra costs of doing business. Furthermore, once loyalty schemes become an expected award, it can be costly and damaging to rattle the loyalty ladder.

Efficiency Economy
Suppliers gain insight into their customers' reaction patterns and thereby define the dos and the don'ts for each specific customer case. This market knowledge can be useful and can

lead to efficient economic initiatives. Often the customer contributes actively to produce efficiency-driven profitability. This can be in terms of communicating needs and wants like volume forecasts, service level indications, engaging in smoothing the administrative procedures such as automatic reordering or correction of errors etc.

Reducing the supplier's quality costs like waste, redoing, more precise points of delivery, insight into habits, routines and service requirements are valuable contributions to improved relationship economy in the trade among the parties.

Chasing efficiency advantages is an ongoing process that takes place over time. Both parties will struggle to attain as large a proportion of the efficiency benefits as possible.

Value-Adding Economy

Sometimes customers participate in, or even take responsibility for, a portion of the relationship value generation. By doing so, the supplier obtains a price premium, larger volume, lower costs, less friction and risk as well as reduced transaction costs.

For some companies, it is an integrated element of a relationship marketing strategy that the customer contributes to the value-creating processes. On consumer markets, active customer involvement can be one of the primary keys to fulfilment of needs, as is the case with do-it-yourself-products where the feeling of creating something yourself is part of the overall experience and is an effective motivation. Electronic 3D interior design, where the consumer can simulate alternative uses of space, furnishing plans and test various decorations in the virtual landscape, offers the same type of value-adding economic benefits.

At the other extreme, there are situations or scenarios where loyalty-based behaviour leads to substantial disadvantages for either the customer or the supplier. Contexts where loyalty is disadvantageous are illustrated in figure 4-2.

Disadvantages for the customer	Disadvantages for the supplier
When it is not likely that the buyer will again purchase from the supplier.	When there is no reason why a seller should ever see a buyer again.
When there is an obvious risk of dependency, and where competitive alternatives exist.	When the seller seeks to avoid dependency of a buyer and where alternatives exist.
When the buying process is governed by non-relationship-oriented processes.	When the selling process is governed by non-relationship-oriented processes.
When the purchase is low-risk and reversible.	When industry ethics make relationship building inappropriate.

Figure 4-2: Non-loyalty-oriented scenarios

4.4 Loyalty in a Market Segmentation Perspective

Loyalty is not a question of either-or, black or white. There are grey areas and complicated, small differences to consider. Loyalty reflects the different degrees of belonging, preferences and decision criteria among customers and target groups. As customer loyalty is a key success factor and therefore a catalyst for competitive superiority, the loyalty factor should in many cases be considered the most relevant market segmentation criteria.

Some basic notions that stress the overall relevance of loyalty as segmentation variable are:

1. When first identified, loyalty segments can be analysed and compared with respect to their attraction: Size in $, volume or numbers, growth rates, accessibility etc.
2. The company's relative competitive strengths and weaknesses can be analysed vis-à-vis each segment identified.
3. Marketing targets concerning positioning can be formulated.

4. Marketing programmes geared towards specific loyalty segments can be formulated aiming at specific goals such as attracting, retaining, and growing through means affecting lifetime efficiency value economics.

Segmentation based on loyalty levels has led some companies to separate customers in the following four groups: hard-core loyalists, soft-core loyalists, shifting loyalists and switchers.[43] An almost identical segmentation model came up with these six loyalty segments: ambassador, core customer, customer, trial customer, prospect and suspect.[44]

The purpose of segmentation is to discover and explore business opportunities. Segmentation without the opportunity angle represents no value. Segmentation criteria should then both reflect distinct characteristics of the market and the opportunity perspective for the marketer.

So, a company or a marketer should definitely pay attention to loyalty segments among customers, but they should also make an attempt to understand non-customers, i.e. customers that are in the periphery or outside the market. Some of these prospects or "suspects" outside the present focus of the actual market served may comprise new, substantial and undetected opportunities. Avis and Hertz have loyal customers based on an airport location concept, whereas Enterprise discovered a completely new rent-a-car market arising from car owners' needs in connection with car repairs.

Another approach takes into account the degree of loyalty and more affective motivational elements. It categorises customers in loyalists/apostles versus defectors/terrorists, mercenaries and hostages.[45] Some industries have succeeded in formulating very beneficial loyalty segmentation definitions. The fine-tuned, graduated loyalty programme practices of airline companies seem rather sophisticated. Typically, they run at least three "mileage card levels", bonus, silver and gold. Each category gives the customer access to various, alternative

Figure 4-3: Market segmentation based on the loyalty pyramid.
Source: Aaker (1991)

peripheral services and prestige levels like quick check-in, gate services, VIP lounges, luggage handling etc.

The loyalty pyramid[46] is a simple, yet convincing, behavioural model to express the idea of loyalty segmentation.

The relationship economy is strongest at the higher levels of the pyramid, because market mechanisms are strongly modified and almost completely eliminated at the top. Hence, one of the purposes of relationship marketing is to *move customers up the loyalty pyramid*. So simple, and yet so difficult. Any product-market and any existing customer portfolio will consist of different loyalty segments or groups. Take motorbikes or cars where the perceived position and key benefits to the customer ranges from transportation to belonging, prestige or identity.

The committed buyer segment is hard-core loyalists with low transaction costs – choosing the role as a monopoly customer – due to factors such as:

- A de facto monopoly-like situation – such as oilrig fire fighting, specialised military equipment or pharmaceuticals.
- Extensive customisation of assets – the customer's and/or the supplier's. A golf club renting the golf course land will very much act as a committed buyer.
- Unique brand equity. Supporters of highly profiled sports clubs, certain life style products, buyers of mission-critical industrial components and management of financial assets e.g. will tend to act as extreme loyalists. One must never forget that one of the secrets of unique brands is that they offer a very strong relationship through the belonging. They create value for customers just by being a strong brand.

For customers in the *product to be a good friend* category, entry and exit barriers to relationships are still high, but not unmanageable. Some of the motives for customers to become soft-core loyalists are:

- Confidence, trust and positive experiences, e.g. suppliers of security solutions.
- High integration in the sense that the supplier's product or service has been designed into the customer's value chain.
- Perceived high quality.

The *satisfied customers with switching costs* have no reason to switch brands or supplier, although they are neither by motivation nor by instrumentality tied to the supplier or the product. Despite this apparent indifference, they are loyal, repeat buyers. If the buyer perceives all competing products in the category to be almost identical, there is no reason to switch. If the buying process is reversible, then low risk, low involvement, and repeat buying routines will save the customer the transaction costs.

The repeat buyer without switching costs and the *price sensitive non-loyal buyer* show rational behaviour if the price is the only relevant choice criteria, because products are perceived to be homogenous and the pure market contract is the usual contractual arrangement. In certain niches within the capital market and in the trading of agricultural products or electricity, where exchanges are organised and handled by intermediaries, customer loyalty is not an issue.

In some bizarre situations, we find relationship-economic disadvantages; reward mechanisms are structured with the purpose of indirectly punishing the loyal customer. Frequent flyer programmes are structured in a way so that mileage or bonus points are granted to the cardholder, usually the business traveller personally. But it is the employer who gets the invoice from the airline. So, companies are being charged a price above the true market price. The firms are involuntarily and without much influence forced to grant their staff an indirect salary increase or a fringe benefit! In this case the customer, i.e. the company, would be better off as absolute anti-loyalist.

Loyalty segmentation in the pyramidal sense can be a pretty difficult exercise. Certain approximating techniques like measuring share of mind (attention value), share of vote (attitudinal value), customer satisfaction surveys and perceptual maps can give a hint about loyalty, but it is otherwise very difficult to gauge.

4.5 Ties and Segmentation

A somewhat different loyalty segmentation technique is to look at the kinds and levels of ties or bonds between seller and buyer, which have a role to play in different contexts.

Monetary ties imply that the customer becomes financially tied to the supplier. Monetary ties can come out of transaction costs advantages – discounts, bonuses, provisions etc – or from the price of core products. As an element in tactical marketing programmes, it is quite common to create exit barriers for customers. Insight into the consumption patterns and ordering routines can be incorporated into procedures and makes repurchase easy for the customer. Such ties represent a certain level of relational-economic protection.

The effectiveness of monetary ties is a balance. If the supplier shares the relationship-economic profits with the customer, monetary ties can be a viable marketing tool. If the supplier exposes the loyalty segment to too much opportunism, the strategy becomes risky. Companies paying above normal prices for travel, just because national airlines have "bought" the loyalty of the employees, will surely break these hostage-like relationships at the first possible occasion.

Social ties: Research has shown that the relationship between two parties tends to remain more or less unchanged despite managerial decisions regarding new policy directions. The informal human networks between the buying and the sales centre have created social organisational ties.

Such networks and informal social relationships are not intentional, as they can lead to dependency. Social networks most often facilitate exchanges and contribute to the generation of positive relationship economic effects, e.g. conflict-solving mechanisms, trust building, risk monitoring and control.

Institutional ties mean that two business systems or organisations engage in a marriage-like relationship. Institutional ties cause very strong loyalty. Facility management, where a company outsources completely functional areas in their supply chain or franchising, where franchisee and franchiser agree on a symbiotic kind of relationship, clearly demonstrates the strengths of institutional ties.

The institutional bonds are in some cases not just the means, but also the purpose of the relationship, as it is the precondition for creating relationship-economic advantages. As a business system, the franchising idea is explicitly built on the concept that the value chain is split up into two independent roles with separate hierarchies, linked together by a comprehensive relationship contract, stipulating concept, roles and responsibilities, key success factors, decision making process and financial guidelines.

When owners of concepts and business ideas prefer franchising instead of forward vertical integration, i.e. multiples or chain stores, it appears as if such a firm sacrifices profits and control to get less financial exposure. The popularity of franchising as a business system demonstrates, however, that the mutual instrumental loyalty created by institutional ties can in fact be a very powerful unification model. Not only because franchise systems allow a healthy, strong motivation in relation to opportunism combined with effective control, but also due to the irreversibility of the arrangement.

4.6 Loyalty Matrix Modelling as an Approach to Segmentation

	Switchers	Fence sitters	Loyal

Customers	Medium	High	Highest
Noncustomers	Low/medium	High	Low

Figure 4-4: The loyalty matrix

The loyalty matrix model categorises the market into segments based on a combination of a buyer behavioural dimension and a buyer relationship dimension.

The loyalty matrix reflects the classical attractiveness-position trade-off, where the customer – non-customer distinction reveals the present *position* dimension of the company, whereas the different behavioural patterns reflect true, generic *attractiveness* of customers in the sense that companies tend to conclude that loyalists are the most attractive customers, ceteris paribus, as opposed to the switchers who are always chasing a slightly better deal.

The marketer will choose the strategic priorities among the different segments in the loyalty matrix, depending on the specific situation. In figure 4-4 – just as an example – a set of hypothetical market strategic priorities is shown for a given company X. The protection of one's own loyal customers in this case has been given the highest priority, as opposed to targeting competitors' most loyal customer base (non-customers).

The marketing logic behind any set of priorities can be challenged. E.g. some companies do not pay much attention to their own loyal customers, as this business is not under attack from outside. Marketing resources are instead invested in retention programmes, often vis-à-vis fence-sitters, in order to increase the level of loyalty or in the acquisition of fence-sitting customers from competitors.

In industrial markets, loyalty is assumed to stem from rational considerations and motives, the subjective and calculated balance between transaction costs on the one side and dependencies on the other. Obtaining low transaction costs often go hand in hand with accepting high dependence. In other words, neutralising the market mechanisms may increase the risk of opportunism. In that respect, loyalty can be viewed as a function of the level of dependence which a customer is willing to live with in order to obtain transaction cost reductions – a sacrifice of autonomy for contribution!

By combining the dimension of *interaction dependence* with *product dependence,* four archetypes of industrial markets can be identified:

The four market cells should be treated as dynamic phenomena regarding customer loyalty. Therefore, a company's portfolio of customers can include relationships of all four kinds at the same time. Consider a commercial bank's relationship with business customers. Some customers tend to act extremely market-like considering the banking services to be like a commodity, always chasing the best prices. Other customers take the more holistic view treating their bank in a cooperative manner.

Customer behaviour might change over the life cycle. In the beginning, customers prefer a more arms-length relationship which in some cases may lead to deep, lifelong partnerships.

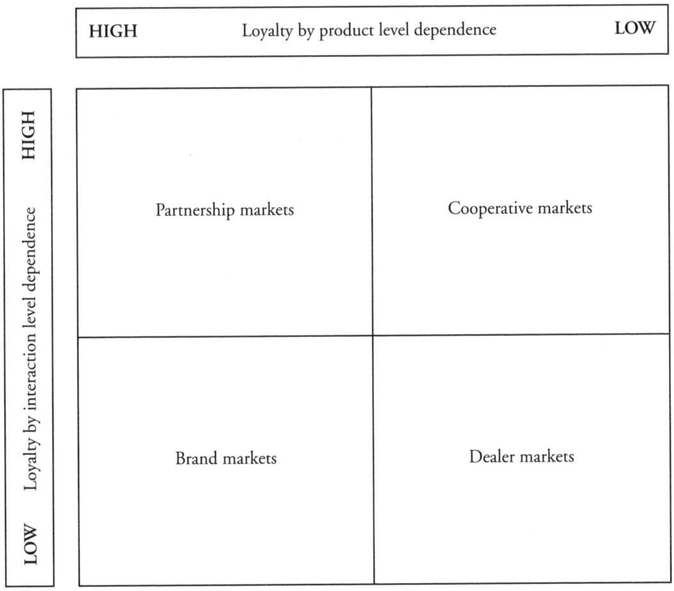

HIGH	Loyalty by product level dependence	LOW
Partnership markets		Cooperative markets
Brand markets		Dealer markets

(Vertical axis label: Loyalty by interaction level dependence — HIGH to LOW)

Figure 4-5: A typology of business markets. Source: Hedaa (1991; 1993; and 1996)

A supplier will try to build customer loyalty by nudging their customers in the direction of dependence. Marketing programmes will either seek to increase the level of interaction in a cooperative direction or stimulate to unilateral dependence through a product or brand preference.

Partnership markets are markets in which customers and suppliers have established a high level of interaction and in which the customer experiences a high product dependence vis-à-vis the supplier. Typically, partnership markets are for highly customised products with high-perceived value for both supplier and customer.

Relationship characteristics in partnership markets are associated with the need for close cooperation between the parties and bilateral loyalty. Not only regarding interaction issues, but also in terms of allocating resources to the relationship. Hence, the level of irreversibility is rather high and the regulating mechanisms tend to develop based on mutual trust.

Brand markets have a relatively low degree of interaction between suppliers and customers combined with loyalty that is derived from a customer perception of high product dependence. Brand markets are often referred to as close to monopoly markets by customers, since they have perceived no or only a few alternative suppliers.

In *dealer markets,* loyalty levels are notoriously low. Dealer markets can be described by a very low level of interaction between the parties coupled with low product dependence from the customer's point of view. Products or services, which are highly standardised, brought to market by equally good suppliers. No complex contact is needed and market contracts are the prevailing regulating mechanism between the parties. The relationships between customer and supplier are purely on an on/off basis.

Co-operative markets are characterised by a high level of interaction between suppliers and customers and are based on a minimum of perceived product differences. Nevertheless, close co-operation between the parties is needed. Contrary to partnership markets, customers do have the possibility of finding alternative suppliers as these are present in the market. Still, switching costs and sunken investments in the relationship give the parties incentive to solve possible problems before considering dissolution of the relationship. Social ties as well as a multitude of human ties within the two organisations protect the relationship.

4.7 Concept to Measure Customer Loyalty

As described earlier, retention, efficiency and value are the three core business-economic terms to pay attention to when analysing the impact of customer loyalty on long-term profits.

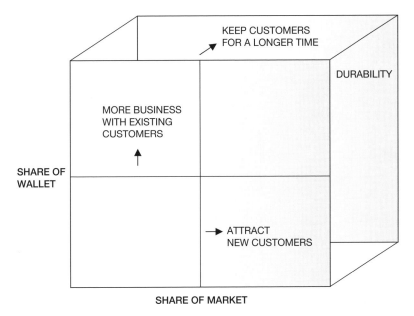

Figure 4-6: The customer loyalty cube

The specific marketing objectives and programmes to be discussed and prioritised in any real life situation could therefore be the *increased durability* of customer relationships, *increased share of wallet* and *attraction of new customers,* as illustrated in the loyalty cube in figure 4-6.

The three different loyalty growth directions – attract through share of market, enhance through share of wallet, prolong through share of life time – do not mutually exclude each other. Very often marketing programmes and sales force efforts are focused on attracting new customers and existing customers tend to be overlooked as the key to growth.

Not all customers contribute equally to the company's profit, actually as well as potentially. The most loyal customers are not necessarily the most attractive target group for a relationship economic loyalty strategy, either. Acquisition may give a higher payoff than retention. Lifetime economics and retention economics must also take into consideration profits and potential.

5. The Driving Forces of Customer Relationships

5.1 The Relationship System

A relationship between a supplier and a customer never exists in a vacuum. Firstly, the relationship is influenced by the participants involved, here referred to as *players*. Secondly, the basic components of the specific relationship have an impact on the life of the relationship in terms of rules, functions, anticipations etc. We will name these basic components the *relationship DNA*. Together, the players and the DNA constitute a kind of relationship cell.

Around this cell, we find other cells or relationships, which the players participate in – directly or indirectly – in the same or in a different role. The relationships are tied together in relationship systems. A vertical supply system is an example of such a relationship system.

The idea of relationship systems can be illustrated as in the figure below.

In the centre we find a relationship cell consisting of players and the DNA cell. Such a relationship is in itself a dynamic force. So is also each of the elements of the relationship. Around the central relationship in the figure, we illustrate how the players are connected with other relationships. The reality is much more complex, but the basic notion is that any relationship is influenced by forces inside as well as outside the relationship.

Narrowing our focus down to the analysis of driving forces arising from the relationship itself means that one must identify and understand the players and their roles as well as the DNA structure. The elements may be illustrated as follows:

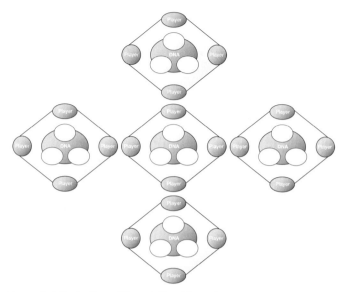

Figure 5-1: Illustration of the relationship system

Figure 5-2 illustrates the two main driving forces of customer relations. The relationship players, the game they play, the rules they follow, their tactics and scope. The four categories of players with a direct impact are the customer, the supplier,

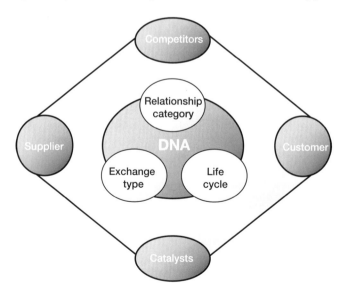

Figure 5-2: The driving forces in customer relationships

competitors and a broad, varied basket of facilitators, and in-hibitors collected under the headline "catalysts". The micro-system represents the driving forces in terms of the player-behaviour with a direct impact on the relationship.

As already mentioned, the relationship DNA consists of the built-in, basic structural attributes of the relationship, which are the exchange type, the relationship form and the embedded, underlying shape of the customer life cycle. These internal driving forces are the basic structures which work un-derneath and influence the outcome of the players' endeav-ours to develop, defend or deteriorate the relationship. At the same time, the players have the possibility of manipulating the relationship DNA.

Like a biological system, almost any relationship in com-petitive environments has opposite forces built into it. *The self-protecting forces* try to legitimize, reinforce and enrich the relationship, while the *undermining forces* constantly chal-lenge, limit, wear and attack its competitiveness and well-being. This organic perception of the relationship, where pressure for growth and protection acts simultaneously and in conflict with constraining and destructive mechanisms, requires further explanation and interpretation. Meaningful marketing initiatives rest on the specific understanding of this pattern of conflicting interaction behaviour and how to cope with it.

Relationships are different in nature, the determinants of life cycle shapes differ, and the level of importance of the re-lationship for the participants is rarely balanced between the parties. The driving force model is a framework for analysis and diagnosis that is applicable across boundaries of different relationship markets. The concept behind this model is that environmental factors and changes are transmitted to the re-lationship via the external driving forces through the arrange-ments made between the players. An exclusive distributor is, for example, exposed to the threat that the principal company will decide to internalise sales and distribution, thereby es-tablishing an affiliate company in the territory. Such action is perhaps initiated as a reaction to strategic moves taken by competitors or as an offensive strike. On the other hand, strong distributors will sometimes be tempted to put a threatening pressure on their suppliers by backwards-vertical integration – establishing their own plants or launching private brands.

Driving forces in customer relationships are by nature difficult to identify, uncover, measure and diagnose. They change over time and interrelate constantly. Isolating the impact of a single element in the driving force model therefore requires careful and patient analysis.

5.2 The Influence Position of the Supplier

Traditional marketing can be seen as a positioning and "monopoly" game in the sense that high market share and dominance efficiency is considered to be an important requirement for high profitability. Introducing mutuality and reciprocal thinking in terms of interactive efficiency and value-driven economic principles changes the ideas of the best long-term position of the supplier. The dyadic motive and the balancing act between the creation of barriers to entry to protect customer relationships on the one hand, and the idiosyncrasy caused by a necessary asset customisation on the other, play a very important role in the new marketing approach for any supplier.

The economic value, and hence the relative importance of a relationship, is often a determinant for the distribution of power between the seller and the buyer. If a specific customer relationship is of high value to the supplier, but is only of minor importance to the customer, the influence of the supplier tends to be limited. The mere existence of asymmetric distribution of power in favour of the customer will as such impede the supplier – the "don't step on the lion's tail" effect.

Small companies with a special competence sometimes get substantial or strategically important orders from big companies, typically in the role as niche subcontractor or development partner. If such an order requires genuine customisation of systems, design, staff, equipment etc., the supplier is put in a difficult marketing situation. On the one hand, the opportunity of obtaining a strategic contract resulting in a competence and reference lift, expansion and perhaps high profitability. All this will imply a higher degree of future strategic freedom. On the other hand, the risk of engaging in an uneven relationship thus gradually weakening the range of future strategic freedom, because customer specific assets represent a low alternative market value and because the exit barriers for the customer are relatively low.

Interdependence of Ties and Trust between Customer and Supplier

The ties between supplier and customer reflect the strength of the relationship between them. When a relationship agreement replaces a market contract, transaction costs go down and the relationship moves into a positive reinforcing circle.

Ties will either be a result of conscious, i.e. explicit, investment strategies deliberately reducing the opportunistic motives of the parties or they arise gradually over the life cycle as a consequence of implicit, tacit adjustments. Hence, we can distinguish between dyadic advantages caused by contractual factors as opposed to advantages derived from incremental processes.

In command situations, as defined earlier, the customer is dependent on or is even a prisoner of the supplier. Such was the case in the early days of photocopying, when Xerox was in a monopoly situation and gave customers service agreement offers that they could definitely not refuse.

In the reverse command situation, the supplier has no other choice than to accept the opportunistic or unilateral moves decided by the customer. In subcontractor industries, such as defence, aircraft building, metal works and certain niches in the building industry etc., this is very often the case. Not only must the supplier cope with fluctuations in demand, price pressure, delays or extensive services. The customer is also forced to take over the commercial risk of the seller, e.g. R&D expenses or investment in capacity in expectation of later sales.

But what if bonds are interdependent? Interdependence does not necessarily lead to a completely balanced fit between buyer and seller strategies. Nevertheless, the parties will tend to develop patterns of behaviour enabling effective adjustment leading to a balanced distribution of the dyadic value creation, depending, however, on how the cards are distributed and the game is played.

The Threat of Vertical Integration in Dyadic Relationships
In any relationship, the influence position of the supplier will vary depending on the risk or opportunity of vertical integration – a joker in a great many customer-supplier relationships.

Forward vertical integration means that a company, typically a manufacturer or a brand owner, establishes its own businesses in finished goods production, wholesale, retail or service, i.e. closer to the end-user. Vertical forward integration represents an opportunity for the supplier and a threat against distributors. *Backward vertical integration* happens when a customer decides to set up a similar operation as its supplier.

The strategic perspective behind vertical integration has to do with either efficiency or dominance-economic aspects, or both. The efficiency-economic consideration assumes that saved transaction costs via in-sourcing exceed the larger production cost, if any. In opposition to this, the market dominance argument is rooted in positioning considerations and premium price opportunities. Some of the most apparent driving forces that stimulate vertical integration in addition to that are:

- Reduction of entry barriers. Lower entry barriers for the customer or the supplier industry influence the risk-return calculations.
- No asset customisation. If the interdependent rela-

tionship relies on non-specific assets, the costs of extrication will be affordable.

- Expected competitor moves. If a company expects competitors to integrate vertically and if the first mover advantages are considerable, some firms tend to take the more offensive step over the doorstep backwards or forwards.
- The quality of existing relationships. Vertical integration can sometimes be a reaction to the opportunism of the trading partner or a lack of motivation to co-operate with regard to specifying assets to genuine needs.

5.3 Competitors as Driving Force

Competition means to challenge, gain and defend relationships. Although the art of relationship marketing is to prevent and resist such competitive pressure, the trilateral forces are what actually keep patterns of trade up in competition. The directions of competition as an influential relationship factor can be classified into four main categories as illustrated in figure 5-3.

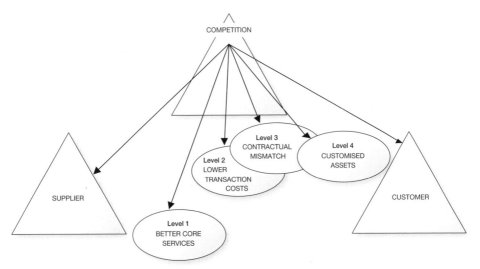

Figure 5-3: Influence of competition on established relationships

Figure 5-3 shows that a competitor can use different edges or "levels" of aggression to shake existing supplier-customer relationships. The higher the level, the more relationship-focused is the strategic move of the competitor.

- Level 1 driver: The core service

Not surprisingly, existing relationships come under pressure if competitors offer better or less expensive core products or services. Strategies built on core services are thus exchange-centric and rely on the assumption that relationship attributes and qualities are just mere supplier tricks aiming at pacifying the customer's rational search for the most competitive solution.

The contrast to this is strategies based upon relationships. Such marketing strategies seek to remove the customer's attention from core services and their generic values, considering them to be trivial, whereas other benefits are incorporated and expected to be determining buying criteria. In the airline business, services like booking, check-in, luggage handling and in-flight comfort are being promoted. In retail, it could be personal service, product exposure, in-store promotions, entertainment and events, interior design, dividend, club concepts etc.

- Level 2 driver: Lower transaction costs

Low transaction costs are a protection mechanism in any customer relationship, as the transaction costs are part of what customers perceive to pay for a product or service. Hence, an offensive strategy aiming at lowering transaction costs can also be an effective tool to challenge existing relationships.

Distribution, logistics, better or faster information, service, product line extension etc. are all key areas that may potentially generate a transaction cost advantage and change the overall competitive picture.

- Level 3 driver: Defeating contractual misfit

In chapter 1, relationships were classified according to the strategies of buyers and sellers in either competitive, command or co-operative behaviour. On this basis, the relationship contract will develop a nature of interdependence, mismatch or dependence. From this we can draw a map of opportunities for competitors to spot and overcome situations of potential mismatch in ongoing supplier-customer relationships.

Figure 5-4 illustrates how competitors can put pressure on customer relationships that are not functioning very well, symbolized as mismatch. The arrows illustrate the competitors' opportunities for breaking a relationship, given the specific established marketing and purchasing strategies. An example: The seller has a marketing approach based on the idea of co-operation. The buyer, however, is not in alignment. The buyer uses competitive measures and will not allow a co-operative atmosphere to gain foothold. The buyer plays hard ball. Whenever the seller puts a bait on the co-operative hook, the buyer eats the bait, but not the hook. Such relationships are characterized by a fundamental mismatch. A competitor will be able to win business through a similar competition-oriented relationship philosophy, e.g. simply by offering a lower price and keeping an arm's length.

• Level 4 driver: Customised assets
Customers often appreciate or even require individual solutions. Instead of offering "one size fits all", a competitor can threaten well-established relationships by offering truly cus-

Marketing Strategies

		Competitive	Co-operative	Command
Purchasing Strategies	Competitive	Independent ←	Mismatch →	Independent
	Co-operative	Mismatch →	Interdependent ←	Dependent
	Command	Independent →	Dependent ←	Mismatch

Figure 5-4: The direction of competitor influence in established customer relations

tomized concepts – not just as a gimmick, but as a vehicle for increased profitability or satisfaction of need in the customer company. Such a move creates disturbance in existing relationship portfolios.

5.4 Buyers and Their Influence

A buyer has two opposing interests concerning supplier relationships, namely autonomy versus co-operation. High autonomy minimizes the level of dependence and hence the negative impacts of idiosyncrasy. We could call this phenomenon the *monadic-competitive* driving force. On the other hand, buyers seek stability, interactivity and smooth exchanges, leading to low transaction costs. This is called the *dyadic-co-operative* driving force. When the level of complexity in the exchange increases, so does the dyadic-co-operative motivation. Buyers demand long term solutions, not just simple exchanges. How these contrasting concerns manifest themselves in purchasing processes and regulating mechanisms depends on a variety of situational, cultural and buyer-specific elements. Most relationships between customers and their suppliers have this mixed atmosphere of co-operation.

Customers can sometimes gain substantial influence over their suppliers by increasing the perception of the relative importance of the specific relationship. Intensifying then becomes a crucial issue in the buyer's supplier relationship strategy as illustrated below in figure 5-5.

The dotted line at the customer-side symbolises increased importance and power in the mind of the supplier.

• Offer a larger share of the budget
In industries with extensive use of outsourcing and subcontracting, companies will often invite their suppliers into closer and more co-operative programmes involving R&D and hence higher risk exposure. In return, the customer offers a larger share of the budget, possibly a sole or preferred supplier contract. The strategic intention of the customer is often to

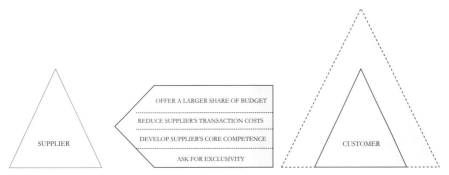

Figure 5-5: Customers intensifying the supplier relationship

increase cost competitiveness thus moving relatively quickly down the experience cost curve by offering the supplier the same opportunity. At a point in time, Boeing reduced the number of subcontractors by 75% in the rivalry with Airbus and McDonnell Douglas. Unit cost calculations were the main argument for the supplier concentration.

Often companies designate a maximum limit for the proportion of a supplier's total revenue they wish to purchase. Such ceilings can disqualify small companies as suppliers. The customer deliberately attempts not to become too influential and not to create a situation of unilateral dependence, image persuasion and lack of control. Therefore, when a hierarchy-like command relationship is about to evolve, customers prefer to loosen the ties to avoid facing costs of dependence imposed on the supplier.

• Reduce supplier's transaction costs
The transaction cost road is an obvious one to follow for a customer as the size of suppliers' transaction costs is heavily influenced by buyer behaviour, such as:

- Must the supplier cope with a bureaucratic, formalistic buying organisation centre and unclear decision-making processes? Or does the customer strive to minimise waste of supplier's time and money?
- How comprehensive are the customer's contractual

routines, i.e. certifications, documentation, legal framework, reps and warranties as well as risk aversion in operational details?

- What are the buying routines at the tactical level? Which and how many competing suppliers are invited to submit bids and how?
- Does the customer have smooth informational procedures in cases of reordering, giving notice, planning for just-in-time etc.?
- Is the quality control level sufficient to reduce supplier costs?

Very often professional purchasers pay too little attention to the transaction costs that arise in the supplying organisation.

• Develop supplier's core competence

Most companies need demanding customers who can actively contribute to the development and refinement of their core skills and serve as references. Some customers might take advantage of this fact and will put a pressure on the supplier's price or loyalty or both.

In many companies, such as IKEA, creating superior and effective suppliers has become a strategic goal rather than a marginal side effect. In relationships where a customer needs a co-operative and value chain-oriented network of suppliers and where the customer's own profitability to a large extent depends on supplier professionalism, the influence of the customer is potentially high.

In industries with short product life cycles, frequent technological shifts and unpredictability, companies are forced to work strategically with suppliers in the R&D phase as solution providers and sole component suppliers. If not, development, design and procurement would be far too slow and costly, as the windows of opportunity are not open for long.

• Ask for "exclusivity"

Customers with exclusive rights tend to be rather powerful

and sometimes even arrogant – a situation most suppliers therefore fight hard to avoid. There can, however, be good reasons for exclusivity claims and the list of such reasons is long: protection against competition, investment requirements, lack of alternatives and strategic impact are among the most common ones. On the positive side, it counts that suppliers can expect a truly committed customer.

How Can the Buyer Motivate the Supplier to Invest in Customised Assets?

Customisation of supplier-assets to one single buyer's needs obviously strengthens the influence of such a buyer. Both because such tacit or explicit investments reflect a co-operative seller strategy and because the outcomes in terms of assets with low alternative market value make the supplier vulnerable. In some situations, customisation is even the core product. Think of a bridge, an airport parking structure, a hotel or a sports arena on perpetual leasehold. The supplier of such fixed asset services cannot very easily re-deploy such assets in a neighbouring county.

The more irreversible and financially immobile a customisation of assets is and hence also the opportunistic temptation, the more comprehensive contractual assurances and arrangements will be requested by the supplier. Trust will rarely be enough of a safety precaution in such situations.
Not only is the supplier heavily influenced by asset customisation – the customer is as well. The local community will hardly threaten the bridge owner that they will switch over to another bridge. Competition does not exist in this relationship.

5.5 Catalysts as a Driving Force

The triad is at the heart of the analysis of the driving forces behind relationships and networks. The triad shapes the dynamic co-optive interaction between customer, supplier and competitors. The simultaneous threat of escalating market mechanisms and the necessary contractual modifications is what constitutes the fascinating framework of competing value chains.

Catalysts represent an independent, multifaceted driving force. From a theoretical perspective, catalysts are the sum of exogenous facilitation, disturbances and "noise" . From the marketer's point of view, catalysts that are present in the close environment are players which actually provoke opportunities or threats to the relationship.

Catalyst forces can be classified into three broad categories of drivers and players affecting a customer-supplier relationship: Complementors, invaders and innovators.

Complementors reinforce and enhance relationships; they provide additional value and stimulate demand.

Invaders are new or established players whose intention is to gain a share of the market by reformulating the relationship parameters.

Innovators are the uncontrolled variety of external parties affecting the competitiveness and sustainability of existing relationships and their underlying strategies without having these relationships as their main purpose.

Whereas invaders is a threatening, attacking element, and whereas complementors ride on the back of established markets and create new demand, innovation is composed of new business initiatives of any kind that might affect ongoing business relations – be it as arising incongruities or missing links.

The Nature of Complementors

Complementarity is an integrated part of the relationship system and an independent driving force at work. A complementor consolidates or expands ongoing customer-supplier relations. Take hardware and software. Better, faster, and cheaper computers stimulate the demand for and the supply of software just because of the new opportunities they create. Software development, on the other hand, pushes the need for new technology, more processing power and desk capac-

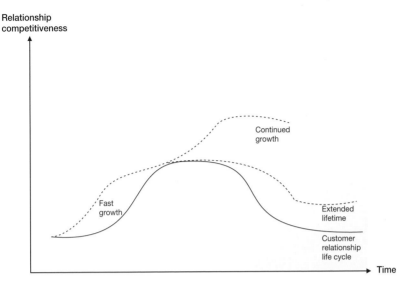

Figure 5-6: The relationship life cycle effect of complementarity

ity. The end result is a never ending positive circle of market increase for both hardware and software.

The dotted curves indicate how complementors facilitate and reinforce relationships. Without complementors, the competitiveness of a certain commercial relationship would grow less fast, mature at a lower level and fade away faster.

Companies should indeed include the often hidden complementors in their market understanding and business planning. Software companies should not just focus on the battle with competitors, but proactively try to match or be one step ahead of what the hardware industry can produce. Big software companies should even try to influence the strategies of hardware manufacturers, which some of them actually do. The same applies the other way around.

Complementors are useful in business relations. In order to get the full marketing impact of complementarity, a company must also adjust its own strategy to create new opportunities for the complementor.

In figure 5-6, the positive influence of a complementor on a supplier-customer relationship is depicted as fast growth, continued growth and extended lifetime. In almost all marketing situations, you will find complementarity – and hence also in relationships. Whereas competition is visible and the first thing in mind for the marketer, complementors are not necessarily that easy to identify and explore. As a consequence, they tend to be neglected or overlooked as a driver.

Invaders Attacking Established Value Chains
Invasion in terms of new entrants increases the intensity of competition and sometimes put the whole industry in a state of alert. They add capacity, they potentially stimulate overall demand, and they most certainly create disruption.

Invaders are different of nature. *Substitutes* are new players satisfying the generic customer needs in new ways through unprecedented business models and consequently offer customers different relationship economic values or variations. They either define the industry differently, apply existing resources in new ways, or they substitute existing business systems by the introduction of new basic elements.

A range of different factors stimulate the appearance of relationship substitution:

- Product and relationship development in other industries not previously related to the supplier industries.
- New technology or new ways of distribution, dramatically reducing transaction costs while increasing the relationship value, respectively, as the case is with video tape compared to a fully integrated digital solution.
- Changed focus among customers.
- New roles and applications.

Invasion by Reconfiguration
A successful reconfigurator may develop a unique selling proposition by rearranging, reinventing or shortcutting supply chains and offering more cost-benefit attractive patterns

of relationships. Some people like the notion of such reconfiguration as Blue Ocean as opposed to conventional configuration in the Read Ocean.

Factory outlets shorten the supply chain from designer-manufacturer to customer. Suppliers of imbedded systems reconfigure the traditional value chain in the computer industry by integrating software into hardware or bundling products. One-stop shops with electronic components and IT have broken traditional borderlines between industries. Reconfiguration is also an option if first mover advantages are obvious.

Innovations – the Driver Beyond the Immediate Playground

We consider the innovative element to comprise such structural external changes or occurrences that can be exploited by the relationship participants to create benefits in the trade between them. New legislation, technology and media are examples of such changes with potential benefits.

Not all suppliers within an industry adapt to external changes and turn them into relationship innovations. In the early days of interactive TV, only a few networks and media communication companies decided to invest in set-top boxes that linked digital and analogue spheres. Interactive TV represents a radical change in the perception and the functionality of the television as media. Set-top boxes and the platform technologies underneath became the enabling factor behind a substantial relationship innovation in the TV and networks industry, i.e. TV as a two-way device.

How can a marketer identify and generate relationship innovative opportunities in the external environment? Fundamentally, there are two different working methodologies. By using the *forward approach,* the analyst is systematically searching for ways to improve well-defined relationship benefits considered to be important for competitiveness, e.g.: "How can we reduce our customers' information costs substantially?" The *backward approach* is when the analyst identifies major external changes, categorises and evaluates them into scenarios, if possible, e.g.: "How could we possibly exploit Bluetooth technology to increase the value of the relationship as perceived by our customers?". In most search-learning processes, there will be several instances where both approaches will be utilised.

5.6 The Relationship DNA

The somewhat trivial statement that the value of relationships > the value of exchanges implies that buyer rationality rests upon a relationship logic that coexists with or even defeats the pure market mechanisms. The behaviour of a buyer in any given purchasing situation is, to a certain extent, also determined by some structural elements attached to the relationship genetics. We call such elements the internal driving forces and have identified the following three:

- *The relationship form.* The relationship form between a customer and the IT supplier tends to develop in a co-operative rather than a competitive or command direction. The relationship is by nature long-lasting and considered important by both parties. The nature of the relationship will often tie the two organisations closer together than the formal contractual arrangement stipulates.
- *The exchange form* in terms of the core product and the natural, "embedded" regulating mechanisms between supplier and customer arising from it. Companies do not replace their hardware and software very often, therefore the exchange frequency is low. During the rare purchasing process, the transaction cost level is considerable. It is not unusual that IT system purchases take quite a long time. It is a very complicated, strategic purchase that involves many people and organisational units all crying out for compatibility, integration in workflow and vice versa, technical support security and many other factors. Furthermore, the buying company will need

ongoing interaction with the supplier throughout
the lifetime of the system.
- *The life cycle form.* At the beginning of a project, a delivery or an ongoing relationship, the parties might
be unaware of the intentions, style and capabilities of
the opposite part, which can lead to somewhat complicated transaction patterns that place weakening
competitive pressure on the relationship. At the later
stages, the relationship may move into long-term stability and informality.

What Impact Does the Relationship Form Have on the Relationship?

The relationship form is determined by the nature of the
product, distribution patterns, as well as technology and industry standards. The relationship form is in no way static; it
will change due to innovations and competitive pressures.

At least four different aspects must be considered in the
evaluation of the relationship form as an internal driving
force and part of the DNA:

The parties
In situations where the likelihood of vertical integration is
minimal, the potential rivalry between buyer and seller tends
to be relatively low. In the opposite case where competition
lurks, the relationship form will develop in a more instrumental control-oriented direction.

The customer needs
Strategic customer needs in industrial markets mean that the
relationship form is of decisive importance to either both parties or just to one of the parties involved.

The car manufacturers have gained significant productivity improvements and cost savings, shortened the production
time, reached higher capacity utilisation etc. through the just-
in-time relationship form; the same goes for the subcontractor as well.

Time horizon

The longer the time horizon determined by the relationship form, the higher the impact on expectations, interaction, specificity of assets and regulating mechanisms.

The communication pattern

Some relationships anticipate intense personal communication, whereas other relationships are characterised by no or very limited personal contact. The supplier and the customer may only have met through the product or service exchanged. In general, interactivity increases the perceived proximity and lowers the transaction costs. In most industries, the increasing level of competitive pressure has forced firms to work in a relationship-oriented manner.

The Exchange Form

We have defined the new marketing concept as company behaviour that attracts, maintains and develops relationships that are mutually beneficial to both supplier and customer. In this respect, it is an imperative to include the core product characteristics in the basic market analysis.

The characteristics of the core product set the scene. Whereas commodities like crude oil, corn or transportation services will be exchanged under pure market contracts, personal or advisory services and other types of highly differentiated products will be transacted in a distinct relationship context.

The core product can in most cases be augmented by enriching the customer-product interface, developing new relationship features like self-service, do-it-yourself solutions, launching of communities, loyalty clubs etc.

The critical influence of the exchange form can be depicted in a simple model, figure 5-7, which shows the dimensions, or parameters, of the core product as a driving force.

The same core product often fulfils rather different needs; the substance and the diversity of needs covered determine the direction and strength of the core service as a driving force

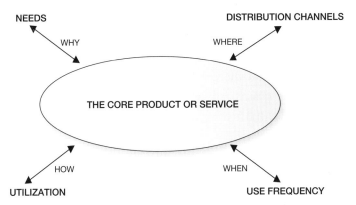

Figure 5-7: The core product as DNA component

for relationships. Take air travel. On the same flight you find both business people, alone or in groups, or tourists that are either travelling alone or in groups as part of package holidays, where the flight is but one element in the total service package.

The satisfaction of the business traveller is influenced by regularity, in-flight service, ground service level, working facilities, space between seats etc. The tourist pays attention to the price. The business traveller is much more relationship-focused than the family tourist.

In many cases the channels of distribution are crucial to the customer relationship. Compare physical stores with web shops. A consumer expects the Internet shop to have lower prices, be open 24 hours and be user-friendly. On the other hand, customers do not expect to get professional personal service, and you cannot touch and feel the products in the web shop. It is easy to click away and you don't have to feel embarrassed leaving the Internet shop without making a purchase.

Use frequency: Light versus heavy use of a given product or service determines what a supplier can and will do on the relationship front. Frequent buyers tend to be more inclined to engage in co-operative framework agreements. Use frequency will often be discriminating segmentation criteria.

The *product or service utilisation* differs. Utilisation can sometimes mirror customer involvement and hence also the importance of the relationship. If utilisation of the product is integrated into the core of the customer organisation or at consumer markets and is combined with high loyalty, the impact can be substantial.

Customer Life Cycle

Among the internal driving forces of the relationship, the customer life cycle is the most apparent. The diffusion of relationship is the underlying force and works in parallel to the dissolution of relationship. Idiosyncratic reactions tend to pull in the direction of dissolution due to conflict of interest and distrust. As opposed to this, the mutual advantages of further exploration or extension of the relationship seem obvious as well.

Some products and services possess the paradoxical attribute that quality and strength erodes at the stable long-time stage of the relationship. When companies break their relationship with advertising agencies after some years of intense co-operation, the reason usually is that communication solutions become less creative and effective, because the parties know each other too well. Adaptation to the attitudes and ideas of the other party might eventually kill creativity and will inevitably lead to conformity and value erosion.

6. Supplier Relationship Levels – Consequences and Contents

6.1 The Ladder as a Relationship Metaphor

Using a ladder to symbolise how relationships develop is not a random choice as the most important benefit of a ladder is the ability to climb up and down, safely and with minimal risk. We will use the relationship ladder to illustrate two important concepts in relationship marketing. The first is that it takes time to climb the relationship ladder. Close relationships don't develop quickly. The second is that the relationship will develop based on mutual exchanges, i.e. a proven track record.

Relationship stages, or steps on the ladder, are used to describe the gradual development and different stages of the relationship. It is worth noting that dissolution of the relationship is included in one of the models, i.e. relationships are not expected to continue indefinitely and may break. Furthermore, the original descriptions of the models all stress that it is important to identify which steps of the relationship ladder are relevant for which customers. Especially important is the total portfolio of relationships, as it may indicate the strength of the supplier, i.e. a majority of high-level relationships will indicate a strong strategic position.

One of the questionable preconceptions about relationship stages is that the higher the stage, the more profitable the relationship is expected to be. As discussed in the chapter on relationship economics, this may not always be the case. Actually, in some industries profitability decreases due to increased investments and costs in relationships that – internally in the organisation – are acknowledged to be of crucial importance.

An important distinction is made between the steps that relate to *traditional marketing* versus *relationship marketing*. The first group of steps includes potential customers and customers that have completed one transaction; the focus in these steps is to acquire the customer and to establish a relationship, if possible. This group is characterised by traditional sales efforts and the initial interest in mutual exchange and making the first exchange, if possible.

The second group of steps includes repeat customers where the focus is on developing and expanding the relationship. Focus will be on enhancing the relationship as a "carrier" of future exchange and ongoing value creation. This group is characterised by ongoing exchange and the gradual development of experiences.

6.2 Five Steps of Supplier-Customer Relationships

Treating customers as assets could indicate that suppliers regard customers as something that belongs to a supplier, but that is not the case. The fact is that it may be exactly the opposite. The implications of this are that the supplier cannot control the customer and that the customer cannot and should not be managed; however, the relationship itself can and should.

Therefore, the supplier should be able to manage the supplier-customer alignment and the relationship with customers. This may prove to be quite problematic, however, as customers pursue different strategies, including some of non-integration with suppliers.[49] This does not exclude the possibility of the supplier managing the relationship and the alignment between the supplier and the customer, but it assigns limits to the possible depth of the relationship.

Organisational relationships between a supplier and a customer is described in 5 levels of alignment, ranging from "spectator" to "partner".[50] The five levels are presented below. The inclination of the supplier to develop a specialised transaction structure is commented on in correlation with each alignment level.[51]

Spectator

There is no sales relationship with the customer. The customer deals with the competitors, but does not see a need for the supplier's products and services, or the supplier chooses not to work with the customer. This level of alignment does not motivate the supplier to develop a specialised transaction structure.

Describing potential customers as prospects or even suspects indicates that the supplier would like to establish an exchange. At this stage, however, neither the supplier nor the customer knows whether or not an exchange will be mutually beneficial. In fact, many sales organisations calculate on using a certain level of non-interested and non-relevant potential customers.

Vendor

The supplier is on relatively equal terms as competitors are, supplying products and services to the customer. This level of alignment may incline the supplier to develop a specialised transaction structure.

Mutual exchange has taken place at this stage. The supplier focuses on how to fulfil the customer's needs and desires either better or more efficiently. Furthermore, the benefits of continued exchanges will be explored as the basis for changing the relationship from a "one among many suppliers" to "one among few suppliers" or even to be a "preferred supplier". The relationship as such will be "under development", but it is important to acknowledge that it is primarily the supplier that is the active participant.

Preferred Provider

One supplier has been chosen by the customer and has the largest total share of the customer's business. The supplier advises the customer with regard to products and services.

This level of alignment does incline the supplier to develop a specialised transaction structure.

This step is characterised by several or a series of transactions that have taken place and are taking place. Both parties express mutual interest and acknowledge interest in developing the relationship. Investments are made specifically to support and develop the relationship, i.e. adjustments or developments of interfaces between the two organisations in areas such as allocation of activities and processes etc.

Business Consultant
The supplier helps the customer to manage part of the business. The customer consults the supplier to meet the customer's long-term business goals. This level of alignment does incline the supplier to develop a specialised transaction structure.

The relationship is now based on the supplier's engagement in the customer's processes and activities geared towards improving the customer's benefit from the continued exchange. We see examples of this in industries where the supplier is responsible for the customer's buying and production planning processes. An example could be electricity production plants and their advice regarding when and from where high-volume customers should get electrical energy.

Partner (Ally)
The supplier manages the customer's business in the supplier's area of expertise providing bottom-line value that cannot be provided without the supplier. The supplier is considered an integrated part of the customer's organisation. The supplier provides completely integrated systems to run the operation and the product mix is often composed of the supplier's products and services as well as the competitor's. This level of alignment does incline the supplier to develop a highly specialised transaction structure.

The specialised transaction structure is idiosyncratic at this stage. Both parties acknowledge the mutual dependency and will at this stage have made internal adjustments in order to accommodate this mutual collaboration.

It is important to note that only four of the five steps actually identify a relationship between the supplier and customer, as the first step is merely a question of relationship initiation.

Hence, just four levels are of interest to relationship marketing as they are the ones that describe the interaction and exchange. Identifying the level of a relationship depends on three indicators related to the five steps of alignment, that is the nature of the relationship itself, the access to different levels in the customer's organisation, and the resources invested by the supplier. This is presented in figure 6-1 below.

Key indicators Alignment Level	Tasks handled for the customer	Access to customer	Resources provided
Spectator	Providing neither products nor services	Limited, usually to gate-keepers	Few or none
Vendor	Providing products and/or services	Limited, usually to lower levels, and to gatekeepers	Product is most important resource – value-added services often provided
Preferred Provider	Providing products and/or services	To low and middle levels	Products and value-added services
Business Consultant	Providing consulting to help customer meet business goals	To all or most levels	Products, value-added services, and consulting beyond products
Partner/Ally	Managing a function of customer's business: often contractual	To all levels	Sharing and managing resources from both organisations

Figure 6-1: Characteristics of the five levels of alignment. Source: Kurzrock (1996, p. 122)

Figure 6-1 illustrates how tasks handled for the customer by the supplier differ, depending on the various levels of alignment. The further down in the figure, the more tasks are handled by the supplier. This is also reflected by the supplier's access to the customer's organisation; the further down, the wider the access. The Resources provided column describes how the exchanges vary in accordance with the alignment level as well.

6.3 Relationships Forms – in a Key Account Management Context

The concept *Key Account Management* has yet to be clearly defined by theorists. However, it is quite apparent that key account management deals with the supplier's handling of customer relationships. The structure of key account management will be introduced later on in this chapter.

The concept *key account management* originated in the IT-sector as the need for treating "key" customers – this typically refers to volume – in a differentiated manner increased. The need arose as a consequence of increased focus on individualisation of the process, designing the offer for the customer, ensuring correct deliveries, implementing on schedule and ensuring a satisfactory execution.

The first positions as key account manager were filled in the late 1960s in the US, often as the visible result of increased customer orientation within the selling organisations. Consequently, staff handling customer contacts was regarded as more important than ever and it became popular to illustrate the organisation with the management at the bottom of the illustration and sales staff at the top, see figure 6-4.

Based on the suggestions above we will use the following definition throughout the book:

Key Account Management is used to describe the supplier's appointment of senior staff that on behalf of the supplying firm is responsible for foreseeing and ensuring the best possible customer relationship. This will preserve the firm's customer portfolio criteria and protect the relationship by developing strong, competitive advantages, efficiently and profitably.

As stated previously, no relationship exists in isolation.

Therefore, it is important to recognise that the supplier's investments and activities concerning each relationship must be seen within a portfolio of relationships. Furthermore, this also reflects the need for comparing relationships in terms of value-creation to the parties involved in the short and the long term.[52]

There are three distinct types of key account management, of which one can be subdivided into two. Therefore, there are four different types to discuss, as illustrated in figure 6-2:

- Contact – one point relationship
- Co-ordinator
- Passive Co-ordinator – customer-reflected relationship
- Pro-active Co-ordinator – supplier-reflected relationship
- Integrator – joint development

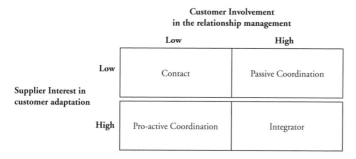

Figure 6-2: The four types as a result of customer involvement and supplier interest

The four types have been tested in a number of different industries and may also be regarded as distinct and often sequential steps when a supplier has decided to invest in managing relationships that has the ability to handle large and individual customer relationships.

6.4 Contact – One Contact Point Relationship

This type is characterised by the task of handling the interface role between the supplier and the customer and is often referred to as "one face to the customer" (see figure 6-3). This low level type of relationship is very common among suppliers that have recently introduced relationship marketing and key account management. There are several reasons for this:

- It is very similar to the traditional organisation of the supplier-customer relationship. The person responsible for the relationship is also responsible for the supplier's sales to the customer
- The supplier's own need for managing the relationship and related information is an important factor
- This type may coexist with a traditional sales organisations (as the need for change is small in terms of changes in responsibility and power)
- The relationship will often be highly dependent upon personal relationships between the people involved
- The need for *new* qualifications is limited
- Recruitment may be internal or external
- Focus of the relationship will be the supplier's sales to the customer

This type is found in industries where exchanges are price-focused. Price focus is often the result for one of two reasons: either there is an oversupply of more or less identical products/services, or the industry does not have any past history of developing relationships. The second reason is characteristic for value systems in which all parties independently handle their own tasks without any interference from others.

All dialogue between the supplier and the customer is channelled through the key account manager as a contact point, i.e. there is no attempt to involve other parts of the supplier's organisation in the relationship.

Customer insights are the responsibility of the key account manager, meaning that information regarding the relationship lies with one individual or, if the supplier uses some kind of customer database system, the information will be accessible to others. Typically, customer relationships are handled in the sales department.

Evaluation of the supplier's outcome of the relationship is based on sales or volume of, in most cases, existing standard assortment of products and services. This is reflected in the choice of key customer, they tend to be large or at least have great potential. As no idiosyncratic investments have been made, typically, there are no entry or exit barriers of any significance. Competitors can therefore establish competing relationships with the customer and may do so without large investments.

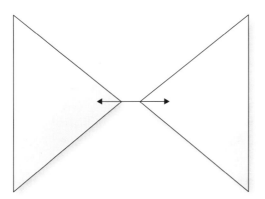

Figure 6-3: Contact – one contact point relationship. Source: Bjerre (1999b)

6.5 Passive Coordination – Customer-reflected Relationship

Passive coordination is a modus operandi for suppliers that have introduced relationship marketing and are experiencing that the customers gradually change from being passive to pro-active. If the supplier does not react to the customers taking over the initiative, it is *passive coordination*. The supplier is basically not interested in adapting either its products or services to suit individual customers, but it must do so due to demands from customers.

Initially, this means that the employee, who is responsible for the customers, has less time per customer and therefore the situation develops into a bottleneck effect. This situation often leads to contacts emerging between the customer and other parts of the supplier's organisation than the key account manager. What's happening is that the customer gradually makes arrangements directly with the relevant individuals in the supplier's organisation, often without the key account manager knowing about it. Gradually, key account management becomes a question of finding out what happened and what has been agreed upon, rather than managing what is actually going on.

The consequence is that the customer is the initiating party, as illustrated in figure 6-4.

This form can be found among firms with some experience in relationship marketing approach. Often firms with experience in dealing with powerful customers or customers that have more insight into the value system adopt this passive coordination tactic. Passive coordination can be characterised by the following:

- Passive coordination is similar to the traditional supplier-customer relationship, but differs from this as it is the customer that is the pro-active party and the supplier that is the passive, or adaptive party
- The supplier's own need for insight may to some extent be limited by the activities of the customer, and in some cases, the customer may know more than the supplier about the value system
- Customer orientation is a result of the relationship, but is actually not desired by the management of the supplier, but must be accepted due to competitor initiatives and customer initiative
- Passive coordination can work alongside a tradition-

al sales organisation strategy, but will gradually challenge existing systems and routines as demands from customers result in adaptations

- The relationship will often be supported by strong personal relationships between the key account manager and the individuals in the customer's organisation, however, this may happen between several individuals in both organisations

- Recruitment for the customer-responsible positions, i.e. account managers etc., may be internal or external

- Focus is on sales to the customer and gradually also on customer profitability as a result of the customer's initiatives and negotiations within various parts of the supplier's organisation.

The responsibility of the key account manager may gradually increase as a result of the customer's initiatives. This may lead to significant differences between the relationships and with customers, leading to decreased standardisation and increased costs of doing business.

Evaluation of success will be based on well-known indicators such as turnover, volume and perhaps even an early attempt to measure customer profitability. Economies of scale will still prevail as the overall goal, as will the standardisation of processes, planning formats etc. This is a delicate balance, as few suppliers do have a financial infrastructure that allows them to assign all costs to the individual customer. Consequently, these suppliers are basically facing the strategic choice: customer orientation vs. standardisation.

As the customer is the initiating party, suppliers often face situations where the customer suggests new modes of collaboration. Sometimes these suggestions may be based on positive experiences from the customer's collaborations with other suppliers, i.e. a supplier may benefit from the investments made by other suppliers having developed new relationship formats or methods. Considerable entry and exit barriers may exist as the suppliers often will have made customer-specific investments. In other words, if a competitor is to enter the relationship with the customer, these investments must be matched.

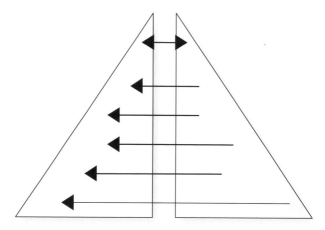

Figure 6-4: Passive coordination – customer-reflected relationship. Source: Bjerre (1999b)

6.6 Proactive Coordination – Supplier-reflected Relationship

This model is based on decisions made by the management of the supplier to use customer orientation to pursue its own goals and to recognise the possibilities of developing strong competitive advantages by developing relationships with customers. Quite often these advantages are based on competitor comparisons, i.e. the advantages are not necessarily advantages in themselves, but become so as a result of comparisons with the supplier's competitors. The increased number of contact points is illustrated in figure 6-5 below.

This form of supplier-customer relationships is found in companies with considerable experience in relationship marketing and a few companies have actually used this form as their first encounter with strategic relationship marketing. Pro-active coordination can be characterised by several points:

- Pro-active coordination breaks radically with the traditional supplier-customer relationship, as it is built around the customer and relevant customer processes

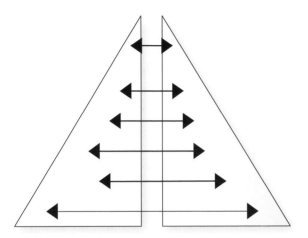

Figure 6-5: Pro-active coordination– supplier-reflected relationship. Source: Bjerre (1999b)

- The supplier acknowledges that the necessary overview of the individual customer requires a close dialogue
- Customer orientation is seen as an opportunity to enhance relationships with selected customers while also outperforming competitors
- This form can, to some extent, coexist with a traditional sales and marketing organisation, but the challenges relating to tasks and processes will gradually increase
- The relationship between the two organisations is supported by the personal relationships between various individuals in the two organisations. Furthermore, one could call the exchange taking place a structured dialogue
- Need for new qualification is quite high as many new areas of exchange are included in the relationship
- Recruitment of customer-responsible individuals, i.e.

account managers, will primarily be internal, as external recruitment will demand substantial resources for training with regard to the supplier's organisation, processes, culture and attitudes

- The role as customer-responsible is regarded as being significant in the tactical and strategic development of the supplier
- Focus will be on developing and strengthening the supplier-customer relationship, customer profitability and the customer's profit from doing business with the supplier. Furthermore, the aim will be to strengthen the customer's competitive advantages at the operational, tactical and strategic level vis-à-vis competitors
- There will be management recognition and interest in investing in the specific supplier-customer relationship, idiosyncratic investments.

Furthermore, pro-active coordination requires highly flexible internal management systems and processes. It is not sufficient to have the interest in strategic relationship marketing, the ability or competency is also necessary.

The customer-responsible individual will often be part of the sales and marketing department. In some instances, suppliers have chosen to establish separate key account departments, often to highlight focus on these customers. In practice, this will reflect the combination of external customer focus and internal competence/department division. More often this is not a "one man band", but a team with members from all relevant departments in the supplier's organisation. The staffing of the team may change over time, especially when the collaboration is characterised by projects.

Evaluation of the success of the relationship will be based on the supplier's and the customer's benefits from the continued exchange, and the impact of the relationship on the customer's strategic goals. The precise common success criteria should be defined and monitored.

The relationship will be based on considerable, mutual investments, specifically geared towards enhancing and developing the exchanges taking place within the relationship. Mutual does not mean shared, but it should be noted that as both parties invest they both take a risk if the collaboration breaks.

6.7 Integrator – Joint Development

The integrator model describes a relationship that is very close. Actually, it is so close that it may be difficult to distinguish between the supplier and the customer in terms of organisation, activities, processes and individuals. The term integrator is an attempt to describe that the collaboration has evolved into integration at least in relation to some exchanges. Please refer to figure 6-6 for an illustration.

It is a model that is most commonly known in industries dominated by large, complex and longitudinal projects. The integrator type is only identified in relation to suppliers that have gained experience by applying relationship-marketing principles. It is characterised by the following statements:

- The integrator model breaks radically with traditional supplier-customer relationships as the customer and customer-related processes are the basis of all activities and processes within the supplier's organisation
- The individual customer is regarded as an individual market (and may be compared to a geographical market in terms of size and priority)
- The supplier will base its own strategic development on close and strong relationships to selected customers and will furthermore regard these relationships as the precondition for outperforming competitors
- The integrator model cannot coexist with the traditional sales and marketing organisation, as the challenges in relation to competencies and processes are

far too great. The sales process also changes considerably, as the relationship comes into focus, the exchanges taking place within the relationship literally take a backseat

- The relationship between the two organisations is supported by the personal relationships between various individuals in the two organisations. Furthermore, one could call the exchange that is taking place a structured dialogue. This will involve every level of the two organisations from clerks to board members
- Recruitment of customer-responsible individuals is only based on internal candidates, as the role is often equivalent to that of a managing director. However, in this situation, the individual is not responsible for the whole company, but for a significant part of it
- As indicated, the role will have significant strategic impact for both the supplier and the customer
- Focus will be on developing and strengthening the supplier-customer relationship, customer profitability and the customer's profits generated by doing business with the supplier. Furthermore, the aim will be to strengthen the customer's competitive advantages at the operational, tactical and strategic level vis-à-vis competitors
- There will be management recognition and interest in investing in the specific supplier-customer relationship as well as idiosyncratic investments. Investments will be planned and evaluated as any other internal investment.

As indicated, the consequences of the integrator model are considerable; both internally and in the way the supplier-customer relationship is maintained. Therefore, it is important to decide which criteria to apply when choosing customers as potential candidates for integrator relationships. With this in mind, three basic criteria must be met:

- They have strategic importance
- They are large or have high potential
- They share the relationship mindset

The integrator form is found in industries where a close collaboration will provide opportunities for product and/or service development. It is important to remember that these relationships will often be exclusive, i.e. it is not possible to have similar or identical relationships with competitors of the customer or vice versa. The supplier and the customer must choose. Describing an *integrator* manager or customer-responsible can be compared to the responsibility of a managing director of a subsidiary.

In terms of the organisational solution, this model often requires a separate department or even a separate location. Compared with the three other models, the integrator model represents managerial challenges, primarily related to internal learning from the individual relationships, which are often confidential.

The integrator model is characterised by mutual investments supporting and developing the collaboration that is quite often shared by the supplier and the customer and based on common specifications. Both face the possibility of losing these investments, regardless of the reason for the termination.

Evaluation of the relationship is based on audits carried out by both parties in full view, as the supplier will know the criteria used by the customer, and vice versa. As indicated earlier, the entry and exit barriers are high and there are serious consequences for both parties if the relationship is broken.

The four forms cover very different types of relationships. Seen from a management perspective, it is important to decide which of the relationship models to focus on. This choice should be based on the supplier's own strategic goals and on an evaluation of the potential customer's strategic[53] goals.

We do not regard any one of the four models to be superior, but market conditions and the specific customer's strat-

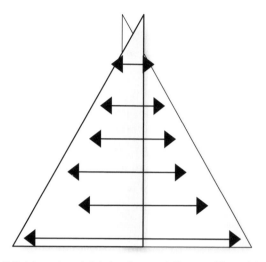

Figure 6-6: Integrator – joint development. Source: Bjerre (1999b)

egy will be decisive factors when choosing the most effective model. Furthermore, it is not a necessity that the supplier changes from the contact to the integrator model, but it is a possibility. Actually, we have seen examples of suppliers that have left the coordination model in favour of the contact model, as a result of changes in the customer's buying strategy and behaviour.

6.8 Relationship Contents

When analysing relationships, it is rarely specified what is exchanged within the relationship. Therefore, a central question is what is actually exchanged in the relationship, i.e. the relationship is primarily a vehicle for exchange and ongoing development of the mutual relationship and business.

With regard to different types of relationships, the level of interaction may differ, and this is also true when focusing on what is exchanged (as further described in chapter 5).

Before discussing what is exchanged, a model to describe exchanges taking place within the dyad will be introduced. That is Ford's definition of "episodes" or specific exchanges or transactions and the relationship atmosphere, which is regarded as the result of a series of episodes. Therefore, a relationship must be regarded at more than one level – as we have earlier referred to as the internal and external level:[54]

- Internal – the exchange between the partners
- Episodes – product or service
- Information exchange
- Social exchange – leading to relationship atmosphere
- Financial exchanges
- Balance – power and dependency
- History and experiences
- Expectations
- External – factors influencing the internal exchange
- Alternative partners – i.e. industry concentration
- Industry dynamics – i.e. trends
- Role in the business system – power and dependency
- Opportunities to change activity sequence in business system

As highlighted in the industry analysis subsection, it is important to distinguish between the short-term episodes and the long-term relationships. This is of importance as the line between what is internal and external may change over time, as the relationship develops and the companies involved adapt and institutionalise the exchange.

However, exchange may also involve external parties or third parties, either supplying one of the organisations in the dyad or both[55]. As described previously, other relationships may influence the specific dyad[56].

The organisations supporting the exchanges taking place are gradually changing from one-way flows to two-way flows to disperse flows (see figure 6-7 below) and from nipple to multiplex relationships.

But what is actually exchanged? Which functions/departments are involved when exchanges take place and what are some of the obvious benefits that these functions/departments may develop from these exchanges? Sales representation and the buying function within the buying organisation is the traditional focus of a relationship and will typically coincide with the conditions for the exchange between the organisations, such as:

- Information regarding product/service
- Information regarding trading conditions and payment terms

The sales representative and marketing department of the buying organisation may share insights on:

- Possible improvements of customer's product/service
- Promotional material
- Product development

The sales representative and logistics department of the buying organisation may design and discuss:

- Improvement of inbound logistics
- Lot sizes
- Forecasting
- Frequency

The sales representative and HRM department of the buying organisation may exchange information and details concerning:

- Training
- Recruitment
- Career development

The sales representative and finance department of the buy-

ing organisation may exchange information and details concerning:
- Payments and payments made
- Planning investments
- Evaluation of financial performance

Remember that exchange may involve more than the traditional two members of a dyad. In order to distinguish between different types of exchange, they have been separated into four distinct classes (see figure 6-7). The four types cover the traditional one-to-one handling of exchanges to the "spider's web", gradually developing from just one line of contact to several lines and into a network.

In principle, the process is simple and quite easy to describe as the organisations move from single contacts to contact-webs.

Uniplex

Uniplex is the traditional relationship and the traditional way of organising the exchange with one representative from each. This is comparable to the contact form of key account management described earlier in this chapter.

The greatest weakness of uniplex is its dependency on individuals in the two organisations. Therefore, efforts to avoid potential loss of information and data will be supported by reporting structures, databases, minutes of meetings etc. Historically almost all this data would be stored individually.

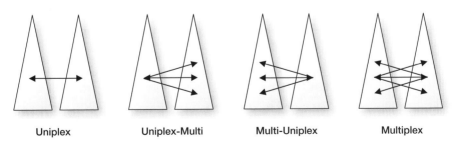

| Uniplex | Uniplex-Multi | Multi-Uniplex | Multiplex |

Figure 6-7: The different combinations of uniplex and multiplex relationships.

The flexibility and the individuality is an important strength, meaning that the individual will often regard the relationship as having personal relevance and will defend it accordingly.

Uniplex to multiplex – One to team

This consists of selling relationships with several functions/ persons in the customer's organisation. This is not necessarily a permanent arrangement, but can be related to projects where desired competencies and insights are part of the organisation handling the exchange.

The coordination of the elements of the relationship and the exchanges, which relate to other parts of the supplying organisation other than the sales department, is a considerable challenge. The individual handling the relationship will be faced not only with a number of questions and issues, but also with choices whether these issues should be handled exclusively or jointly.

One risk is that the balance between the supplier and customer will become uneven and one-sided, i.e. that the customer takes over the initiative or simply occupies the individual representing the supplier with demands. This is comparable to the passive coordination form of key account management described earlier in this chapter.

Multiplex to uniplex – Team to one

This is the opposite situation from Uni to Multi, but basically the problems are identical. The buyer handles relationships with several functions/persons in the supplier's organisation and is faced with the same challenges and choices as the seller in the Uniplex-Multi relationship.

Coordination of the internal elements of the relationship and the exchanges therein is only handled by one of the organisations involved; the buying organisation. This is comparable to the pro-active coordination form of key account management described previously.

Multiplex – Team to team

Multiplex relationships mean that several representatives represent each company involved. Tacit knowledge may develop within the group and both organisations will often attempt to share experiences internally and aim at best practice.[57] The drawback of this is that it may be difficult to share experiences with individuals outside the relationship.

The team-to-team approach may be institutionalised further, for example by devoting parts of the company solely to handling the relationship with one partner. Tacit knowledge develops within the group and across the organisational boundaries, often working within its own set of boundaries and practices. Supporting the relationship by developing a unique organisational structure could develop into an independent company. Thereby moving into limited merger situations where the companies decide to share some of their competencies and resources.

Finally, when looking for external factors of considerable importance to a relationship, you must never assess your own value to your customer or to your supplier. Basically, the following tough questions must be answered: Could the three areas in which we provide our customers/suppliers with value/benefit be obtained anywhere else? Or put another way: What is the result from our relationship that cannot be copied?

7. Relationships in Different Environments

Industry Characteristics and How They Affect Relationships

Relationships do not exist *per se* and they are not necessarily beneficial to any of the parties involved! The environment influences whether relationships may develop as well as their characteristics. This implies that the relationship will partly reflect the external conditions within the industry in which the partners of the relationship operate.[58] Thus, there is no such thing as the "perfect" relationship, but rather relationships that are formed and developed under various forms of external and internal constraints.[59]

The guidelines on how to analyse an industry are included in several textbooks on marketing. This section is based on the "Noble Art of Industry Analysis",[60] which outlines a three-step approach as described below. However, prior to this analysis, the question of defining industry boundaries must be addressed.

Industry analysis, or the definition of an industry, basically builds on the customer needs that are satisfied by the company's product or service. Another way to define the boundaries of an industry could be geography, i.e. the North American car industry, products, i.e. dairy products, or operational mode, i.e. the franchise industry. The boundaries are important, as they reflect the unit of analysis. Furthermore, the industry defined by customer needs may allow for identification of potential competitors that do not provide the same product, but who fill the same need. For example, when decorating a home, the manufacturers of lamps are competing with wallpaper manufacturers, paint manufactures, etc.

In principle, an industry analysis will provide a static and up-to-date description of the situation, which may not be sufficient to evaluate the market potential. Therefore, the analysis should be supplemented by considerations about future developments and trends in the industry. If one were to look at internet-based sales of fast moving consumer goods at this point in time, the numbers are not impressive; however, expectations for future revenue are extremely high. Assessing the effects of changes in the industry is difficult, partly because changes are hard to foresee and partly because effects of changes are not always apparent. One way of handling this would be to try to answer the following question: "What could change the way we do business today to the extent that we could no longer sell our existing products/services?" To answer this question, the three-step approach may be applied:

I   – Customer's competitive situation which is closely linked to the traditional analysis of industry attractiveness

I   – The relationship value system – may be compared to the business systems analysis, and

III – Potential competitor analysis.

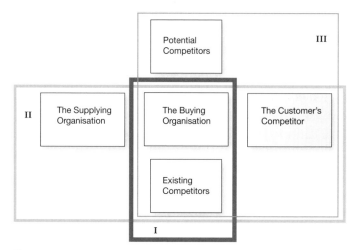

Figure 7-1: Industry analysis – the three-step relationship approach
Source: Inspired by Hayes, Jenster and Aaby (1996, pp. 123-148)

I – Customer's competitive situation (industry attractiveness)
This first step will ascertain the level of profitability and this level may give an indication as to whether or not it would be interesting to invest in a relationship with a customer in this industry. If profitability levels are high, the inclination to invest in relationships is high, as it is of strategic importance in order to ensure access to the business system, which the customer is part of. Furthermore, if profitability levels are high in one part of the business system, that part may look for opportunities to expand its role in the business system by adding more functions and/or activities.

If profitability levels are low, it may not be attractive to invest in relationships as it would be difficult to identify the benefits for the selling organisation. However, in this situation, it is expected that organisations in the industry may look to suppliers to assist in increasing industry attractiveness, either by relationship development or by enhancing competition among suppliers.[61]

II – Relationship value system (business system analysis)
This analysis reveals the critical and unique parts of the value-creation, as seen from the customer's point of view, in the business system. The analysis of the business system will also reveal the distribution of power between the organisations involved in terms of critical components in the value-creation process.

Relationship development will focus on the access to these critical components and to being more reluctant towards the non-critical component, if these can be separated.

III – Potential competitor analysis
This form of analysis here identifies the strengths and weaknesses of organisations in relation to the industry performance levels, the components handled in the business system and in relation to each other or what can be termed as a relative assessment of strengths and weaknesses. Thus, the concept of power is also part of the implications of this step.

Relationship development in this phase will then focus on the winning customers if the functions and activities in the business system are expected to remain unchanged. However, if the business system is in a transitional phase or is undergoing radical change, relationship development may focus on the organisations where changes in the business system are expected and welcome.

One might pause to ask, have you performed an industry analysis on customers, suppliers or even your own company? Few companies do this, primarily because the workload is considerable and because it may be difficult to invest in the resources necessary.

These three steps are examined in more detail in the following three subsections.

7.2 The Buying Organisation's Competitive Situation

Analysing the competitors of a customer often provides relevant information related to the strategy, policies and behaviour of that specific company, especially in terms of manoeuvrability and potential. Key elements of competitor analysis are the assessment of the following characteristics:

- Strategies pursued by competitors – basically identifying cost focus and/or differentiation focus, serving many or few segments, acting as the innovator or follower, etc.
- Market performance – which implies a description of the players in the industry, their size, their market share, product and service range(s), price, customer relationships and a description of their use of distribution channels
- Operational performance – in terms of use of resources, use of production capacity and factors such as human resource management, organisational structures, recruitment

- Financial performance – searching for key drivers of economies of scale, economies of scope etc.

The central point of competitor analysis in the context of strategic relationship marketing is to evaluate the relative strength of the partner in the partner's industry.

The status of the competitive situation may be supplemented by a future scenario by generating strategic options for the competitors and thereby be able to assess the SWOT of the customer in focus. If the relationship develops, you have to realise that your partner's strengths are an important part of the relationship's potential and your partner's weaknesses are important parts of the relationship's challenges.

In order to accurately evaluate a customer's potential for future development, it is also important to analyse the attractiveness of the industry, which the customer is part of. As seen from a supplier's point of view, it is also a question of choosing where supplier resources are expected to produce the highest profitability.

The key issues to assess when evaluating industry attractiveness in a relationship are as follows:

- *Profitability* – the financial return on capital compared with competitors to the industry, i.e. is it worthwhile to invest at the moment?
- *Growth* – the opportunity to grow businesses organically by keeping up with basic demand, or is growth acquired by mergers and acquisitions?
- *Size* – must be large enough to be "significant" to "serious players", i.e. economy of relationships must be attainable.
- *Customer/risk* – the more customers, the less risk (see the following section on industry concentration)
- Is it possible to identify *potential for changes* in these first four elements due to closer relationships to specific customers in the industry?
- *Barriers to entry* – specifically the analysis of the po-

tential for investing in customised assets and thereby creating difficulties for new players looking to enter the industry due to capital requirements, special competencies, existing relationships between players in the industry, capacity, etc.
- Characterising the *relationship climate* in the industry – is there a risk of opportunism in the industry?
- *Capital intensity* – the relative amount of capital required to support revenue stream(s): the more intense, the less attraction.

Industry attractiveness may turn out to vary, depending on the industry of the observer. It is worthwhile to note that attractiveness may vary at different levels of the business system. For example, an industry may have many suppliers of raw materials, but few production plants, or few manufacturers of computer chips, but many potential customers who produce computers and other electronic devises using computer chips.

The industry attractiveness analysis may prove to be of great importance when assessing the supplier's interest in future relationship developments as illustrated in figure 7-2.

7.3 Relationship Value System

Traditionally, analysis of a business system was based on the deconstruction of the system into separate activities and identification of the sequence in which they are performed. Taking it a step further, it is then possible to link the sequence-critical competencies and critical resources necessary to perform these activities. This we label the "Outside-in Perspective" in the relationship value system.[62]

The business system is defined by the organisation in question, its existing competitors, its suppliers and its customers.

An example of a relationship value system is the media surveillance industry serving its customers by providing news clippings and news summaries – acquiring news channel access, identifying articles and other points of interest to customers, clipping, organising themes/clusters of news, writing summaries, editing summaries as well as packaging and bundling themes/news.

When analysing the business system, the primary component is the individual activity performed. Initially, it is not a question of who does what, but what they do. Having identified the components, they are then placed in the sequence in which they are performed. It is important to note that it is common that business systems display more than one linear sequence of components, i.e. these may be loops, parallels, doubles (identical sequence copied) or even pauses. Some of these sequences may be performed by different organisations in the business system or within the boundaries of a single organisation.

It is important to stress that the value system analysis is dynamic. Therefore, it is not sufficient to analyse the existing business system, but it is as important to identify changes and trends affecting the business system as well. The dynamic part of the analysis may also provide value for the potential relationship partner as the selling organisation may play an important part in realising changes and new sequences of functions and activities in a modified business system, as is performed in detail in the potential competitor analysis.

Knowing and understanding the business systems, within which a buying organisation plays a part, is important when considering what aspect to focus on in relationship development.

However, another approach to industry analysis is identifying value creation in the business system, focusing on scarce resources[63] in the system, such as competencies,[64] tangible and intangible assets or asset specificity.[65] This analysis is based on the combination of these resources and assets and the output of these. This will often illustrate a whole range of output in which the industry in focus may have a large share. This is labelled the "Inside-out Perspective" of the business system[66].

Implications of the inside-out perspective are primarily

that existing relationships may develop into others based on valuable competencies and resources applied outside the industry's boundaries. With regard to the earlier example of the media surveillance industry, the inside–out approach would ask; can competencies and resources be used in relation to other partners or other products or services? Or more specifically; can resources and competencies, such as having offices open at night, staff working at night, knowledge of the individual customer preferences and interest areas, packaging, journalism, writing skills etc., be used elsewhere?

The important point is to ensure the reader's knowledge of more than just one way of defining competition for competencies and resources. Furthermore, the "Inside-out" approach has the advantage over the "Outside-in" approach as it originates from the company in question and not from an analytical point of departure open to all competitors.

Furthermore, it is important not to stop at dyadic relationships, but also to focus increasingly on value systems that combine a number of companies. This development runs in parallel with Supply Chain Management and some new in approaches could be outsourcing or third-party partners or maybe even fourth-party partners.

7.4 Potential Competitor Analysis

Analysing the potential competitors of a customer, who will also indirectly be in competition with the relationship value system, may provide insights related to how the customer's customers may be served by different value systems. It is important to note that this analysis goes beyond the existing competitors as they are part of the first step.

- Potential competitors are identified by using the findings in step II – Relationship value system to basically identify the value delivered by the business system no matter if it is serving many or few segments, acting as the innovator or follower, etc.

- Once the value is identified, the search begins for alternative ways to deliver this value. In principle, this is a classical analysis of customer benefits that is supplemented by an analysis of the alternative value system's strengths and weaknesses.
- Once the alternative value systems have been identified, the search for competitive advantages, vis-à-vis these value systems, begins by searching in all processes and activities of the relationship value system. These may be found in:
- Market performance – the key success drivers' size, market share, product and/or service range(s), price level and/or range, investments in developing and retaining customer relationships, or in use of distribution channels.
- Operational performance – in terms of the use of resources, use of production capacity and factors such as human resource management, organisational structures, recruitment.
- Financial performance – the key drivers of economies of scale, economies of scope etc.

The central point of the potential competitor analysis in a relationship business context is to evaluate the relative strength of the customer in the customer's industry as well as the relative strength of the relationship value system compared to value systems outside the customer's industry.

The status of the competitive situation may be supplemented by future scenarios in order to generate strategic options for the potential competitors and thereby be able to assess the SWOT of the customer in focus. If the relationship develops, you have to realise that your customer's strengths are an important part of the relationship value system's potential, and your customer's weaknesses are important parts of the relationship value system's challenges.

Combining findings in the customer's competitive situation with findings in the relationship value system analysis and the potential competitor analysis leads to a matrix illustrating where to focus on relationship development and where not to. These considerations are summarised in figure 7-2.

Relationship Value System Strength

		High	Medium	Low
Customer's position vis-à-vis competitors	**Strong**	Invest in relationship or growth	Protect and improve relation and profit	Exploit relation- and improve profits
	Medium	Improve relationship and profitability	Ensure relation	Invest only to harvest and reduce costs
	Weak	Focus on profit, not on the relationship	Avoid investments or development of relationship	Prepare to exit or slow wind down

Figure 7-2: Prioritising where to develop relationships and with what purpose

This matrix suggests where to invest in relationship development and where not to. It also suggests the purpose of relationship development. The combination of high relationship value system strength and the strong competitive situation of the potential customer suggests investment in relationship development with the focus on growth, i.e. go with industry leaders and assist them in maintaining their position. However, a combination of low relationship value system strength and the weak competitive situation of the potential customer suggests that investments should be withdrawn from the relationship as neither the industry nor the potential customer appears to be attractive. As illustrated above, the spotlight is not on industry analysis per se, but on the strategic decisions related to relationship marketing, with special focus on the impact of the customer's strategic situation.

7.5 Industry Consolidation

Industries often share "paradigms" for relationships in terms of type and content. In some industries, such as telecommunications, joint ventures are sometimes formed between competitors. In this way, relationships among competitors can exist and develop across organisational boundaries.

In other industries, such as the ice cream industry, competition is fierce in the local as well as international markets. Situations have occurred where ice cream manufacturers have physically removed the freezer and its contents of its competitor from several retail outlets and replaced the freezer and its contents with its own brand. Therefore, relationships between competitors are not possible in this industry.

Besides industry characteristics[67] supporting these paradigms, the concentration of the industry also plays an important role as to how relationships develop. The industry concentration is located in the outer environment. Industries can also be described in terms of market share distribution or concentration as well as the number of companies that exist within the industry as a whole, as illustrated in figure 7-3.

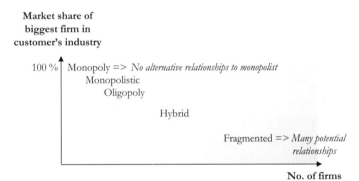

Figure 7-3: The industry consolidation continuum in the customer's industry

Figure 7-3 indicates whether or not a supplier has the choice between many different alternative relationships, or if the supplier is more or less forced to establish a relationship with the only customer in the industry. This is merely to ensure that we discuss the supplier's interest in developing relationships with a customer in the industry concentration context, as will also be discussed under the "monopoly" heading; do we have a choice?

Monopoly

This type of industry is characterised by just one organisation dominating the market or as is often the case, the industry may be labelled monopolistic when there is one very big organisation and several small ones.

Smaller companies will constantly challenge the market leader, either through lower prices or through specialisation in serving niches or segments also labelled *segment nippers*.

The expected relationship[68] strategy in this case would be to develop relationships with the dominant market leader. However, market dynamics may suggest relationship development with one or more of the challengers as well, depending on the assessment of the market leader's SWOT and response profile. If the market leader is strong, it is absolutely necessary to develop a relationship if opportunities in the industry are to be examined. On the other hand, if the market leader is weak, relationships with the market leader should be kept at a minimum so as not to hinder the development of strategic relationships with the smaller organisations where the potential is high.

Suppliers to many European telecommunications industries face situations like the one outlined here. That is when the national markets are dominated by the original and often state-owned organisations. This is also the case with many national airline industries in Europe.

Oligopoly

This is when only a few large organisations dominate the customer's industry. Often these organisations serve different consumer segments, i.e. intra-industry competition is limited and they rarely compete head-to-head.

In relationship terms, the limited intra-industry competition implies that it may be possible to develop relationships with all these organisations at the same time. However, the contents and the structures of the relationships may vary considerably depending on the potential partner's strategy. Relationships beyond the operational level may be mutually exclusive, as strategic relationships may be used as a basis for future competition.

The international airline industry is an example of an oligopoly, where many organisations serve several airlines, for example airline catering at a specific airport. But when it comes to developing new menus or new dishes, or even more radical elements such as developing new food processing techniques, the relationship often becomes strategically oriented and therefore results are not shared outside the dyad.

Hybrid

Hybrid industries are characterised by some medium-sized, some small and some developing organisations. Market dynamics are often high and changes are frequent.

At this level, industry concentration competition is intense, and it may be quite difficult to develop simultaneous relationships to organisations within the industry, as they can be difficult to handle. Competing organisations may demand either exclusivity or guaranties of confidentiality. This situation will force the selling organisation to be careful when choosing which organisation to approach first, second, third, etc. as relationships to these "first choices" may prevent the development of relationships to other organisations.

As is often the case, many examples of "real-life" can be found in the middle of the relationship development continuum. This is also the case for the hybrid level of industry concentration. Examples of such industries are advertising and communications, retail, furniture, among others.

Fragmented industries – in principle close to "perfect competition"

Here, basically no industry concentration is observed. All organisations in the industry are small in terms of market share. The competition is typically fierce, margins are generally low and the search for lowered production costs is intense. Very few organisations will attempt to pursue a differentiation strategy in order to fulfil niche demands.

Relationship development at this level of industry concentration will typically be based on a low investment approach and a desire to re-use solutions and processes in as many relationships as possible.

One example of a fragmented industry is the metal shops that serve the windmill industry. Although the metal shops may desire to develop tighter relationships with a specific producer, the producer does not see the need for this, as the risks of not having a relationship are considered to be minor.

The different levels of industry concentration summarised above all describe a static situation. However, most industries are in a constant state of flux either at a slow or fast pace. The consequences are that the level of industry concentration may change, or that the conclusions regarding the individual organisation may change, i.e. that an organisation previously considered to have a strong position has become weakened or vice versa.

Industries in transformation pose a more intriguing problem as this raises several questions seen from a seller's point of view. Actually, the points stressed below are equally relevant to buying and supplying organisations. These issues specifically concern the business system, i.e. the division of activities in the industry. Basically, an organisation may change the business system in four different ways:

Active approach to industry transformation
- Take-over – Acquire the partner
- Change – Choose another partner
- Do-it-Ourselves – Develop the process, the resource etc. ourselves

Passive approach to industry transformation
- Wait – Let the battle be fought – waiting to see a winner

These options address key elements of the company's own strategy and how the organisation perceives itself. But they also emerge from your partner's point of view, i.e. in times of transformation, the uncertainty increases and choosing which relationships to enter into and which to break can be very difficult.

Take-over

This step requires that a take-over is considered as a strategic advantage to include the activities and processes of the partner. Reasons for this may include exclusivity of the output and competencies of the partner, or it may focus on potential benefits stemming from improved coordination, improved exchange etc.

Change

Choosing another partner is dependent on the existence of other potential customers, and that these potential customers are also interested and willing to do business with you. This is where the identification of future winners among potential partners is necessary.

Do-it-Ourselves

This means building and developing the necessary competencies and capabilities within the organisation. Evaluating this will often be a "make or buy" decision, applying economic tools and principles.

Wait

This is the patient method. Keep cool and let the process of "natural selection" go undisturbed. In terms of relationship marketing, there is not much strategy related to this approach.

One of the ways of coping with change is to try to lock-on to the development among the company's customers, i.e. to develop and nurture relationships with the winners among your customers. This is how LEGO has decided to cope with changes among their retail customers around the world. Lego's statement with regard to the realisation of its goals is:

"We will achieve our goals by growing with the leading customers".

The LEGO example raises another important question, namely the geographical reach of the relationship. This may be a decisive factor as costs of match and content of match must be investigated. Some of the levels of the geographic reach are:

- Local – typically a one-to-one company relationship
- National – often a one-to-one company relationship
- Regional – often a several-to-several company relationship
- International – typically a several-to-several company relationship
- Global – always a several-to-several company relationship

Global relationships are present among a number of multinational corporations (IBM, ABB, DHL, Siemens, Procter & Gamble, etc.) which are organised into a lobby called a Global Forum. They meet to discuss how global relationships may be improved simultaneously from a supplier as well as a customer viewpoint.

An interesting point in these discussions is the focus on one relationship at a time, i.e. although they spoke of "programmes, systems and the like", nothing is standardised to the point where the specific characteristics of the individual partner are set aside.

7.6 Relationships in Digital Value Chains

Virtual value chains change the whole marketing environment. The value of a network is its functionality. That is the ability to distribute, store, assemble, utilise and modify information. Networks combine richness and reach of information[69] and create an atmosphere of power in relationships based on information distribution. Therefore, a network where partners do not share intelligence in the dyad is not likely to gain competitive strength.

Both the marketer and the customer will try to capitalise on what is called *intelligence migration strategies.*[70]

Arbitrage:

Because intelligence can be located anywhere in a network, there is often opportunity of moving particular types of intelligence to new areas where the costs of maintaining the intelligence is lower. These are typically labour-intensive operations.

Aggregation:

As intelligence decouples, companies will have the opportunity to combine formerly isolated pools of dedicated infrastructure that can be provided over a network. Consulting firms do so through curriculum vitae databases and personal competence profiles. Portals such as Netdoctor.com (health) and Smartforce (e-learning) have the aggregation of knowledge as their value proposition.

Rewiring:

In essence, this strategy involves the creation of an information network that all participants connect to and the establishment of an information exchange standard that allows participants to communicate. Virtual office solutions enabling people to work together on the same project, sharing documents and background information is an example.

Reassembly:

Another new kind of intermediary creates value by aggregating, reorganising and configuring disparate pieces of intelligence into coherent, personalised packages for customers. This is the case with a company called Morningstar. Morningstar collects a comprehensive amount of data from and about investment funds. Morningstar measures funds using

80 different benchmarks. The collected data are sold to the investment funds as in-frames, advisor tools, ratings, co-publishing etc. Morningstar adds reassembly value and the funds are both suppliers and customers – the dog eating his own tail!

Digitalisation is a puzzle for companies across industry boundaries. No one can avoid the disturbances, which can be both opportunities as well as threats, in the transition to virtual value chains. If relationships are like diamonds, one could ask: Are diamonds forever or will virtual value chains gradually erode the concept of loyalty?

7.7 Relationships Across the Industry Life Cycle

Having discussed the industry attractiveness and concentration, the business system and possible changes due to digitalisation as well as competitor analysis, it is now time to turn to the development stage of the industry.

The actual stage of the industry life cycle tends to influence the inclination to develop relationships, especially strategic relationships. Therefore, there are links between the stages of the industry life cycle and possible relationships.

But first the concept of power must be considered as power is one factor discussed in connection with relationships. The presence of power centres may be the reason for developing a relationship even when there are not necessarily shared interests per se. Power centres can be quite diverse and can be discussed in terms of size, resources, expertise, information, future potential, etc.

A one-sided relationship[71] is when one party forces the other to enter and maintain the relationship, despite the opposite party's intention. At best, the one-sided relationship is beneficial to one party and without negative consequences for the other.

Power as a concept has been defined earlier, but the way power may support a one-sided relationship is as follows:

- *Size* – the customer has a large share of our business, and we cannot afford to lose this business. Often very important in companies basing their performance on economies of scale
- *Resources* – the supplier has a monopoly on certain resources or plays a significant role for our value creation
- *Expertise* – we cannot do without the specific element/item/component – an example could be Intel microprocessors
- *Information* – we need to know what is going on in our customer's business – or at the next level of the business system
- *Future potential* – we cannot develop our business without the relationship as the partner is regarded as a first mover
- *Future winner* – we stick to the winners of the future – if they survive and we have a relationship with them, then we survive too.

	Price Competition	Brand Loyalty	Overall Rivalry	Relations
Embryonic	Low	Low	Low	Why bother
Growth	Low	Low	Low	Developing
Shakeout	High	High	High	Strategic relevant
Mature	Low/medium	High	Medium/high	Strategic interest
Decline	Low/high	High	Low/high	Strategic cash cow

Figure 7-4: Relationships related to the industry life cycle. Source: Modified from Hill and Jones (1992)

It may be assumed that relationships develop as the industry does. Industry development stages are defined in the following section.

Embryonic
Embryonic industries are characterised by low or no price

competition as there is a customer or demand surplus in the industry, i.e. customers and demand is plentiful. This is, of course, related to the identification of undiscovered needs or the fulfilment of known needs superior to present offerings.

As most players in the industry are new, and thus unknown and without a reputation, there is low brand loyalty as few preferences have developed among customers. References do basically not exist and the level of information uncertainty is rather high.

Limited competition between the organisations in the industry is reflected by the low level of rivalry that exists, i.e. resources and production have not yet reached the level of full capacity and the demand exceeds the supply.

At this stage in the industry life cycle, a central question is: "Why bother with developing relationships?" Furthermore, at this stage everybody will have a chance to survive the following stages of development and it is far too early to identify winners, their strategic behaviour and the competencies and assets they posses. This may be a cynical approach, but what can be done about it?

Although relationships at this stage of industry development are rarely close, experience shows that they may have considerable impact at later stages. This is an extremely important point, namely that relationship development also should be seen in terms of *path dependency*. This path dependency once again reflects that a relationship rarely exists without any external influence either current or historic. This form of dependency will therefore reflect all past exchanges and the way in which the involved organisations and individuals behaved along the way. Actually, there is a parallel which can be drawn from our own lives; that this concept works the same with personal relationships as some develop positively and continue to do so, while other relationships deteriorate either gradually or abruptly.

Growth

As the industry expands its supply, more and more customers

see that their needs and desires are fulfilled. However, demand still exceeds supply and price competition is low.

The industry is still young and the brand awareness is low, as is the loyalty towards these brands. The primary reason is lack of experience with the individual brand and insight into comparisons between the brands and the organisations behind them. Rivalry between members of the industry is low, primarily because the winning strategies in the industry have not yet revealed themselves clearly.

The industry will gradually approach equilibrium between demand and supply. This means that the overall rivalry in the industry will be low, except in specific areas such as special competencies, use of patents etc. where this may be different.

Developing relationships become more visible as they gradually emerge between companies who share a collaborative strategy and who also share a willingness to devote resources to relationships. Another type of relationship may develop, i.e. the one-sided relationship, as attempts to develop relationships are carried out. Relationships are thus characterised by a strong belief in and expectation of future benefits.

Shakeout

As competition increases and the supply gradually exceeds the demand, rules of the game will change. Price fluctuation will often be the first reaction to increased competition, and the secondary set of reactions is that the players will begin to look outside their organisational boundaries to identify opportunities of cost reductions.

The third set of reactions is often to focus on differential opportunities, i.e. where it is possible to differentiate offerings to the customers. This will lead to an increased or at least emerging interest in customers' preferences and investigations into where and how relationships may be established. Differentiated market offerings may gradually lead to brand awareness and brand loyalty.

Competition will, beyond price, also be dependent on

who gets which business with which customers as the level of rivalry increases. Therefore, some of the players in the industry will begin to look beyond their borders to identify opportunities for differentiation and value-creation.

It may become strategically relevant to develop relationships when the battle really begins in the industry. Gradually, the companies setting the pace in the industry emerging are separated from the followers. During this process, the company must aim at the potential partners with an optimal fit.[72]

As the winners will take it all, it is crucial to identify the winners and to identify generic winning strategies and the related Key Success Factors. The focal point of analysis should be where we, together with our customer, could strengthen the *relevant key success factors*. At the same time, it is important to identify areas where a relationship basically would make no difference and thus to stay away.

Mature
Mature industries typically display either low or medium price competition, depending on the size of the exit barriers, as the remaining firms have often settled in terms of maintaining customer demands. This reflects the situation where there is low or medium rivalry between the organisations as they focus on optimising their supply to the customers rather than acquiring new customers.

Reputation and experience exist between suppliers and customers, i.e. high brand loyalty is quite common.

Mature industries tend to possess common understandings or paradigms for how relationships exist and with what content. Mature industries are often characterised by strong strategic interest in developing and maintaining relationships. This is also important as changes in the industry are slow and when changes take place, for example when one supplier is replaced by another, it often has considerable impact on the supplier that loses the relationship. Relationships are very important at this stage of the industry life cycle, and often to be regarded as strategic assets.

Decline

Declining industries may display both low or high price competition and rivalry. It depends on the capacity and the exit barriers within the industry. In some situations, organisations leave the industry due to lack of future potential and such industries may continue to be profitable for the surviving organisations. Such industries will display high brand loyalty, at least among the remaining customers.

Industries in decline must be regarded as strategic cash cows and existing relationships should be protected. However, investing in new relationships or expanding existing ones does not seem to have strategic impact or make sense.

8. The Individualised Approach to Relationships

8.1 Typology of Strategic Behaviour

Within the strategy literature, we find a number of typologies that focus on how firms should react to the outer environment.[73] There have traditionally been two different foundations for these typologies: one has been based on theoretical arguments leading to e.g. the model of Competitive Advantages,[74] and the other has been based on empirical studies aiming at describing what has been observed.

Using typologies for analysis should always be carried out with caution, as a typology cannot describe all characteristics of an organisation. But the central point of a typology is that it helps to bring order in an incredibly cluttered conceptual landscape.

Originally, the typology of strategies pursued by firms was based on three empirical studies. These studies covered different types of organisations and the goal was to develop a general typology that would be applicable in different areas of economic life. The typology was narrowed down to four different archetypes of relationship behaviour. A second aim was to present a typology describing various adaptation patterns for organisations. Both purposes have been fulfilled[75] in a clear-cut and forthright way by discussing several cases and examples.

The result of the original empirical studies was a typology with four archetypes, namely *Defenders*, *Prospectors*, *Analysers*, and *Reactors*.

A central concept in the typology is "Fit" which is used to describe the alignment between the strategy pursued by an organisation, the organisational structure and its management processes. Successful firms are well-aligned and therefore the strategy, structure and management processes "fit" together in an optimal way. These elements within less successful firms, however, do not work as well together and therefore do not "fit" as well. The degree of fit will also reflect the organisation's ability to pursue consistent strategies, meaning that low fit implies that some parts of an organisation aim at objectives and goals that are not necessarily shared by other parts of the organisation. Seen in a relationship context, this means that it is difficult to develop close relationships to all parts of an organisation having low fit, whereas this is possible with an organisation with high fit. The concept of fit is partly a description of process and partly of situation:[76]

> "... a dynamic search that seeks to align the organisation with its environment and to arrange resources internally in support of that alignment. In practical terms, the basic alignment mechanism is strategy, and the internal arrangements are organisation structure and management processes. Because in a changing environment, it is very difficult to keep these major organisational components tightly integrated, perfect fit is most often a condition to be striven for rather than accomplished."

Within each archetype, an adaptive cycle exists. An *adaptive cycle* is the organisation's ability to change in terms of product, market domain and technology. The reason for looking at the adaptive cycle is the dynamics it represents, i.e. the strategic archetype does not merely characterise the organisation, but also the way the organisations react to changes in the environment.

The basic principle of the typology is that it is possible to identify a pattern by the way organisations move through the adaptive circle and at the same time solving the problems and making the necessary decisions.[77] How this takes place differs, depending on the strategic archetype. The adaptive cycle is illustrated below in figure 8-1.

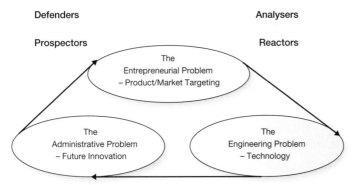

Figure 8-1: The adaptive cycle. Source: Based on Miles & Snow, 1978, p. 24.

The entrepreneurial problem deals with the choice of product(s), market(s) and domain(s) i.e. the choice of specific product(s) or service(s) and target market(s) or market segment(s). This is not a one-time problem, but one that continues to play an important role in the organisation's continuous passing through the adaptation cycle process. The adaptation cycle process is defined as an organisational capability that influences the degree and type of change, which the organisation can handle at any given time as related to choices of products, markets, and technology. In a relationship context, this will influence the areas of focus for the relationship as well as where the customer looks for support from its suppliers in order to serve the chosen market(s) with the chosen product(s). This deals with relationship content and the question of what is exchanged.

The administrative problem here deals with the reduction of internal insecurity and the creation of stabilising elements that will support future development of the company. Thus, internal processes are key areas. In the relationship context this is where the exchange between supplier and customer could focus on enhancing the customer's internal processes, improving forecasts, utilising competencies and assets etc. In terms of required information, the administrative problem calls for intimate knowledge and insight into the customer's processes, activities and decision-making structures.

The engineering problem deals with the creation of a system that supports the choice of product and market. Thus, this area is related to the choice of technology for production and distribution. Development of suitable control and information systems is a key part of the engineering problem. In a relationship context this is where the supplier may be able to influence the infrastructure of the customer's operation.

As indicated earlier, the different strategic archetypes may pass through the adaptive cycle in different ways, resulting in different strategies. In the original typology,[78] two clear-cut opposing strategic types were identified: defenders and prospectors. Defenders are characterised by their consistency and by isolating themselves from the outer environment, as opposed to prospectors, who are characterised by a continuous change of procedures and structures.

However, a combination of the two opposing types was also identified: the analysers. Analysers are described as a compromise between defenders and prospectors. Consistency and renewal thus characterise analysers. A fourth type was, somewhat reluctantly, also identified:[79]

"... the Reactor,[80] exhibits a pattern of adjustment to its environment that is both inconsistent and unstable; this type lacks a set response mechanism which it can consistently put into effect when faced with a changing environment. As a consequence, Reactors exist in a state of almost perceptual instability.... Thus, the Reactor is a residual strategy, arising when one of the other three strategies is improperly pursued."

The unit of analysis is the concept of *customer's organisation* as a whole. It is therefore important to go beyond the superfluous level of analysis if the strategic type is to be identified and not merely analyse one or two parts of the organisation in question.

8.2 Defenders – It is All About Costs

Typical for organisations of this type is that they have a relatively narrow product and/or market domain. Furthermore, the decision-makers in these organisations consider the environment to be simple and stable. This leads to a managerial focus on only a few indicators in the environment and no focus on indicators that do not directly impact the internal operations or the domain in which the organisation is active. The managers in defender organisations may be characterised as follows:[81]

> "Managers in Defenders usually restrict their perceptions to a narrow range of external stimuli, which are expected to influence the organisation (mostly related to technological developments). Typically they allocate a small amount of administration and staff to monitoring other organisations, events, and trends. In addition, environmental scanning is performed only by a few top executives of their staffs."

As defenders view their environment as relatively stable and simple, they focus on "doing things right" once they have identified what the right things are. Another consequence is that managerial focus is primarily internal and with emphasis on the engineering and administrative portion of the adaptive cycle.

In other words, they will stick to their strategy and their positioning as long as possible and will only change when they acknowledge that the environment is markedly different from their internal dominant perception. This also means that there is no intention of involving others in the decisions related to the entrepreneurial part of the adaptive cycle. The main focus is on cost efficiency of internal distribution and production systems. For defenders, low price is a central issue in their marketing strategy and their positioning.

The long-term strategic goal is to maintain the position of cost leader as compared to competitors and it should be noted that all initiatives that potentially may help sustain this goal could be of interest to a defender.

Relationships to suppliers are, generally speaking, not regarded as beneficial, but as boundaries that limit the defender's management options to choose among potential suppliers and customers, depending on where the best deals can be made. Relationships therefore concern the administrative and/or the engineering part of the adaptive cycle, but are not considered to be of strategic importance. However, it should be noted that relationships are generally regarded as limiting the management's ability to control the organisation.

Defenders are well-known, for example in FMCG-retailing, and a perfect example is the German retailer, Aldi. Aldi relies heavily on advanced systems for scanning, control and follow-up. The defined key measurement factors are for example: SKU coding, turnover per hour, turnover per employee, etc. Other key factors are: DPP and Space Management which is used and managed internally, systems that create the basis for simple operations and the ability to use low qualified staff. Information is only shared with suppliers and only if it suits Aldi. Collaboration is used to minimise Aldi's net costs in terms of handling, transportation, storage, shelving, interest, etc. Suppliers have to adapt to the retailer's systems and processes. Positioning is based on low cost, secondary locations, standard inventory, efficiency in terms of refilling shelves, pallets that can be driven directly into parts of the sales area, stores that are almost 100 % identical and, if possible, the retailer prefers to design the location as opposed to accepting an existing one.

8.3 Prospectors – It's Got to Develop

Prospectors are opposed to defenders as they constantly seek new opportunities and attack the existing and dominant perspective in a business sector. Thus, prospectors look for new positioning opportunities, focusing on the outer environment. The prospector can be described as:[82]

> In order to locate new areas of opportunity, the Prospector[83] must develop and maintain the capacity to monitor a wide range of environmental conditions, trends, and events.
>
> The Prospector, therefore, invests heavily in individuals and groups who can scan the environment for potential opportunities. One means of spotting and exploiting opportunities is to develop and elaborate surveillance capacity by decentralising and scanning activities to appropriate sub-units within the organisation.

The prospector strategy reflects a high level of initiative with regard to the environment. The environment is seen as changing and thus constantly providing the organisation with new opportunities. The organisation develops new products and undertakes new initiatives and is therefore highly focused on the entrepreneurial part of the adaptive cycle.

The outer environment is considered to be complex and characterised by constant change, and therefore new initiatives must constantly be tested. These new initiatives will typically relate to the positioning, regarding the administrative and engineering parts of the adaptive cycle as instruments supporting the initiatives. Internal flexibility and dynamics are key capabilities.

A prospector's long-term goal is to be *the* innovator of the industry they are part of or to redefine the industry and the way the supply chain functions. Several of the well-known prospector organisations have done exactly this.

Relationships are regarded as beneficial as long as they can keep up with the development pace of the prospector and as long as the relationship does not limit the possibilities of developing other relationships. Relationships are considered to be of strategic importance to a prospector when related to the entrepreneurial part of the adaptive cycle. This does not imply that prospectors do not have other relationships, just that these are not strategic.

One prominent example of a prospector is SONY whose CEO has been quoted as saying: "My most important task is to ensure that we through our own product development are able to make our old products obsolete before our competitors do so". Other examples of prospectors would be Apple Computers in the IT-sector, Amazon.com redefining bookstores and other "first movers" in an industry. Apple's launch of the iMac is a brilliant example of changing the way a product looks, the colours it can have and, of course, the whole idea of making the product partly transparent. Apple has also been involved in setting up their own retail operation and the unsuccessful result of this stresses that prospectors take risks, often great ones.

8.4 Analysers – Rather Be Safe Than First

Analysers play it safe and they can be characterised as a combination of cost- and risk-minimiser (defenders), and opportunity seekers (prospectors). Therefore, analysers are often organisations that are one step behind in terms of innovation, but are nevertheless often organisations that their partners can rely on and that have clear positioning within their market.

This is possible due to the division of the organisation in two, the base part providing the majority of income and the development part that is used for trial and error activities. External stimuli are transferred to the base part, after proof of the significance in the development part of the organisation. To do this successfully, analysers rely on other organisations to lead the way; thus, they follow in the footsteps of prospectors if these developments are applicable within the base part of the analyser's organisation.

In an analyser's outer environment, there will be a number of prospectors from whom analysers can detect new business opportunities. It is important to note that the analysers often have a global perspective on prospectors in their markets, i.e. an analyser may be the first to introduce a new product or service in a market, having noted the success of a prospector in another, typically geographic, market.

The analyser's norm for cost efficiency is that of the defender. This will apply due to the innovative delay of the analyser as compared to the prospector, which gives the analyser the opportunity to analyse how the strategy should be pursued as related to all three problems of the adaptive cycle. Analysers thus typically copy and follow the prospectors, but ensure that a positive result is not jeopardised by new initiatives.

The analyser focuses on all three parts of the adaptive cycle and it is important to note that the analyser is the type where the frequency and the speed of the adaptation is by far the highest of the four types. Furthermore, going through the parts of the adaptive cycle is often regarded as a process in itself. An analyser is quite conscious about continuously monitoring changes internally and externally, in particular focusing on the successes and failures of competitors and colleagues internationally.

The use of all parts of the adaptive cycle also implies that it is possible to develop strategic relationships that concern each part of the adaptive cycle.

An analyser's long-term goal is often very clear in terms of positioning and vision of how to get there. They know what they want. The consequence of this is that analysers often engage in relationships, especially if these relationships support the overall strategic developments of the analyser.

Examples of analysers would be organisations such as IBM, Maersk Sealand, and General Motors. These firms share the motto: "We would rather be safe than first" and encourage thorough analysis and caution.

8.5 Reactors – Let's Move

Reactors are "followers" in the sense that they react to new trends from competitors by attempting to duplicate the success of the competitor, but do not have the managerial systems or capabilities to analyse or investigate why and how competitors do what they do.

Reactors survive in stable industries or in industries where competition leaves room for organisations that do not exhibit superior performance or focus.

The result is that they do not pursue any consistent strategy or development path and will apply any possible technique or tool, if they have the impression that others are doing so successfully. This type of behaviour is very open to input from others and can change existing routines.

Reactors are organisations that stick to earlier successful business models and they will typically end up in a situation where they are not able to choose a positioning strategy with regard to price, quality or innovation. Thus, they do not focus on specific products or markets.

All parts of the adaptive cycle may be considered equally important and changes are often decided upon as a result of desired changes in other parts of the adaptive cycle, i.e. changes in the IT processes are a result of needs in the entrepreneurial area. Therefore, strategic relationships may be developed in areas concerning all parts of the adaptive cycle.

Basically, a reactor does not operate within any decisive timeframe and therefore a relationship to a reactor may serve as basis for new developments, testing new products or services, testing new ways of co-operation etc. The possibilities are almost limitless. Generally, relationship development with other partners is regarded as a way of ensuring vital inputs such as information, competencies or as a catalyst for change.

Examples of reactors are typically found among the COOP's in the dairy industry, farmers and retailers, which is due to internal structural problems in the administrative part of the adaptive cycle as well as the lack of internal clear priority of goals and means. They are caught between the interests of the organisation, i.e. the need for funds to invest in product/service developments, production facilities etc., and the need to financially satisfy their members in terms of the highest possible prices for production inputs, dividends etc.

The implications of the four types are illustrated in figure 8-2 focusing on what part of the adaptive cycle is most relevant to the development of strategic relationships.

Differentiation Focus

	Low	High
High	*Defender* Short-term focus Administrative and engineering part of adaptive cycle	*Analyser* Long and short-term focus Entrepreneurial, administrative and engineering part of adaptive cycle
Cost Focus		
Low	*Reactor* No time focus Entrepreneurial, administrative and engineering part of of adaptive cycle	*Prospector* Long-term focus Entrepreneurial part of adaptive cycle

Figure 8-2: Areas in which strategic relationships can be developed

The consequences of these four types can also be expressed in terms of what kind of benefit a supplier may get from developing relationship to these customers, i.e. are the customers interested in developing relationships, and if so, what would be their primary focus? This is outlined in figure 8-3.

Differentiation Focus

	Low	High
High	*Defender* Will pursue flexibility – avoid investing in specific assets Rationalisation Focus of lowest possible specific transaction cost	*Analyser* Investing in specific assets Coping with customer "cherry-picking" Partnering projects Focus on lowest possible specific transaction costs and specific developments
Cost Focus		
	The sellers Transaction Cost Leader Strategy will be applicable	The sellers Transaction Cost Niche Strategy and/or the Quality Segment Specialist Strategy will be applicable

Figure 8-3: Consequences of the four types in terms of their focus and the seller strategies that may be successful

	Reactor Testing new ways of working and processes developing new forms Educating new staff Focus on lowest possible generic transaction costs	*Prospector* Product development Process development Investing in specific assets Partnering projects Focus on creativity and innovative skills
Low	The sellers Relationship Differentiator and/or Transaction Cost Leader Strategy may be applicable	The sellers Quality Segment Spcialist Strategy and/or Relationship Differentiator Strategy may be applicable

The intent of introducing the typology of strategic behaviour was to classify different types of behaviour and different strategic needs and opportunities related to the individual organisation. But in order to take the individualised approach to strategic relationship marketing a step further, a framework for assessing the importance of a potential partner, as seen from the potential partner's point of view, must be introduced. Cron and Levy (1987) have attempted to describe the consequences of the four types in terms of sales management focus. The buying organisation's perspective will therefore be adopted when discussing whether or not to engage in strategic relationships.

8.6 Strategies Related to Buying

Buyers or buying organisations segment their suppliers just as suppliers segment their customers and ultimately these segments contain one organisation. This statement seems to surprise many sales and marketing organisations despite the fact that this situation comes up quite often. The introduction to supplier segmentation has been developed within the Supply Chain Management (SCM) framework, which in principle is geared towards:

> "...the integration of business processes from end user through original suppliers that provides products, services and information that add value for customers.[84]"

And in practice this means:

"The management of upstream and downstream relationships with suppliers and customers to deliver superior customer value at less cost to the supply chain as a whole.[85]"

Of course, not all relationships are equally important or have equal impact on business processes within the supply chain. Therefore, most buying organisations focus on getting the most out of their, often limited, resources. One increasingly used approach[86] is to prioritise resources and choice of focus based on the risks associated with co-operation with a supplier, as perceived by the buying organisation. The risks are evaluated both internally and externally.

Internal risks are those that:

- May cause potential loss of profit, due to:
  · Lack of delivery
  · Quality deficiencies
- Have high importance of delivery, as they are crucial to the ongoing production
- Incur set-up costs in case of re-starting the production – could involve costs for cleaning, waste due to … etc.
- Have high complexity in terms of delivery and degree of mutual integration between the supplier and the customer.

Internal risks are all related to the internal consequences of the supplier's failure or inability to fulfil contracts and/or other obligations.

External risks are related to:

- The number of suppliers
  · Potential in terms of ability to fulfil needs
  · Those that can and want to deliver in terms of abil-

ity to meet the needs and demands of the customer
- The entry barriers for new suppliers, the higher the entry barrier, the greater the risk
- Negotiation strength of the supplier(s), the relative importance of the customer to the supplier
- Degree of commodity in the delivery, the more standardised, the lower the risk.

External risks are all related to difficulties and risks of exchanging an existing relationship between the customer and a supplier.

If the internal and the external risks are divided into low and high risks, and combined in a matrix, the result is as illustrated in figure 8-4. This table illustrates the rationale, as seen from a buyer's perspective, concerning where to focus and where to engage in strategic relationships with external partners.

		Internal Risks	
	Low		**High**
High	Bottleneck materials and services	Strategic materials and services	
External Risks	**Ensure supply** (Automated procurement)	**Partnering** (Co-operation and integration)	
	Non-critical materials and services	Synergy materials and services	
Low	**Hands off** (Auctions)	**Encourage compteition** (Marketplace portal)	

Figure 8-4: The customer's segmentation of suppliers. Source: Based on Krajlik (1983)

When risks are high, internally and externally, strategic relationships may be developed due to the importance and consequences in case of failure. The aim of the relationship is to ensure the supplier's attention and interest in continued co-operation.

When either the internal risks or the external risks are considered high, it may also be possible to develop strategic relationships. However, in a relationship strategy perspective, it is important to remember what the purpose of the relationship is, seen from the buyer's point of view. High internal risks combined with low external risks will encourage relationships that are focused on the administrative and especially the engineering parts of the adaptive cycle. As opposed to this, low internal risks combined with high external risks will encourage relationships focusing on the entrepreneurial part of the adaptive cycle.

If both groups of risks are considered to be low, it is difficult to claim that strategic relationships are a necessity. The modern[87] buying approach is based on the buying function's role in realising the strategic goals of the organisation.

The term "supplier management" has also emerged within SCM literature[88] as a way to enhance product development, smooth out order and buying processes with regard to invoicing and payments. The main task within supplier management is supplier development, i.e. developing a profitable and strategic relationship to the chosen suppliers as these relationships are regarded as the basis of increased productivity, quality, flexibility, innovation, and process alignment. As an interesting parallel to the supplier's focus on key customers through key account management, a number of buying organisations have developed key supplier managers to ensure focus on key suppliers. As indicated earlier, the SCM concept does not apply equally well to all four strategic types of behaviour, especially not to the defender strategy.

This development has been phrased "Buyer Initiative" as it is seen in a classical marketing context[89] where it is quite often the customer that chooses the supplier, and not the other way around as is typically taught in traditional marketing courses.

9. The Sales Centre

9.1 A New Perspective on Sales and Relationships

Building, developing and maintaining supplier-customer relationships is no longer an individual accomplishment – but based on a team effort. Therefore, we regard key account management and other organisational structures that support supplier-customer relationships as being based on team accomplishments. However, it is not merely a question of organisational structures if the company is to match the customer's buying centre – it is also a question of what resources and competencies are required to do so. And how should responsibilities and empowerment be organised in order to support the organisational structure in the creation of a unique supplier-customer relationship?

Sales-wise, it is interesting to know what kind of attitudes and behaviour you can expect from different personalities/personality types. Once you are able – at least in most cases – to properly identify the actual type, the members of the sales centre will be much better equipped to handle the various situations that may arise in a supplier-customer relationship.

In order to get the most out of understanding the members of the customer's buying centre, it is relevant to understand one's own personality and ability to accommodate for this and be flexible when interacting with others. The customer – as a whole – must perceive the supplier as trustworthy and as a potential partner for further mutual involvement in collaboration – rationally as well as emotionally[90].

Team Selling
Handling the buying centre and the customer-specific solu-

tion requires more resources and the involvement of more competencies than ever before – and this development has just begun and will be even stronger in the future.

Continued customer demands to innovation will further enhance demands towards providing competitive edge. Customer expectations are increased quality, real technological advantages, more innovative products and solutions, higher productivity and more comprehensive solutions – often at lower prices or lower investments than previous solutions.

These customer expectations – and demands – increases complexity; especially when building, maintaining and nurturing supplier-customer relationships vis-à-vis prioritised customers. To meet these expectations, the quality and competencies of the members of the sales centre have to increase – especially if the relationships rest on the shoulders of a few (or even one) individual(s). New success criteria arise, the depth of the supplier-customer dialogue increases, and focus gradually turns from sales to underpinning and developing the customer's competitive edge and competitive force.

In many instances, the supplier-customer relationship has resulted in the supplier building "exit-barriers" for the customer, forcing the customer to stay in the relationship, because the costs associated with leaving the relationship are considered to be too high, too difficult or simply not worth the trouble of getting a new supplier-customer relationship aligned.

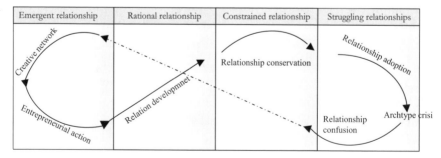

Figure 9-1: Know your customer, at an organisational as well as a personal level

An important trend in sales and relationship strategy is that the importance of personal relationships is diminishing – personal relationships may still be decisive, but many other factors play an increasingly significant role. These could be external factors, but also the number of individuals that are involved in the relationships and the transactions will increase the complexity of the decision-making process.

Widening the supplier-customer relationship opens new business opportunities as new contacts and new types of exchange emerge – benefits will be commercial and personal:

- Developing and implementing concepts and solutions creating increased efficiency and improved performance
- More refinement and conceptual competency development amongst team members
- Increased understanding of business system for all parties involved
- Increased market cap for all team members
- Increased diversity in the work
- Improved market position for the organisation
- Access to ideas and know-how amongst the participants involved
- Joint competitive edge

9.2 Conceptualising Team Selling

Team selling is a way of working and is an integrated part of the delivery system and the delivered value to the customer. Therefore, not all customers are eligible for this approach as the resources required are considerable. There must be an (quantifiable) expectation of the outcome and/or potential outcome of the specific supplier-customer relationship – at least in the long run, but preferably also in the short run.

Team selling can be regarded as either a necessity in order to match the customer's expectations of advice and strong conceptual solutions, or as a way to differentiate the supplier vis-à-vis competitors. No matter what the motive is, the sales process will become more complex and demanding.

Sales processes often take a long time – and on one side this implies that the dependency of the individual employee will diminish, although at the cost of increased internal co-ordination and communication. I.e. new challenges show up when the sales process takes more time – there is no such thing as a free lunch.

A very important question is whether or not team selling is relevant to all sales organisations. Based on the demands for resources and competencies indicated earlier in this chapter, there will be situations in which team selling is not value-adding – on the contrary, it may be too expensive and confusing. Therefore, we have listed a number of indicators that – if fulfilled – would indicate that team selling is appropriate:

- Complex products/services
- Individualised deliveries to the customer
- Cross-category relevance to the customer
- Longitudinal sales process/buying process
- Sales process that involve several independent entities, i.e. partners, VARs, distributors, etc.
- If the customer's buying centre has several – identified – members
- If the sales/buying process involves several hierarchical levels in the customers organisation (maybe the supplier's organisation too)
- If the sales/buying process involves several functions/departments in the supplier's organisation.

In other words, selling commodities will probably not call for team selling, especially not if these commodities are sold as standard products according to standard trading terms.

However, still fewer "standard sales processes" occur, which is why team selling may be relevant in both large and small teams. Teams may be divided into various types of teams, i.e permanent versus temporary teams (sometimes referred to as "ad hoc"), and generalised versus specialised teams.

But before going into depth with the team selling principles and approaches, it may be valuable to consider how to match the team with the customer's buying centre and to consider which competencies are needed in the team.

Setting the Team Scene

Setting the team scene – and choosing the person responsible for the team – is a critical and important decision for the supplying organisation. It is not merely a question of matching resources and competencies; it is also a match of personalities that is required.

Imagine a large corporation in which a number of individuals have developed strong and close relationships to relevant contacts in the customer's organisation – how would they react if the priorities of the corporation changes and they have to turn their focus elsewhere? Being able to communicate internally and explaining why priorities have changed and why the individual persons will have to change focus in order to bring more/higher value to the corporation is a key competence for the person responsible for the team.

As responsible for the team, it is not just a question of having the financial responsibility; it is also the responsibility for the strategic development of the supplier-customer relationship. So, the team has to match not only the required resources and competencies vis-à-vis the customer, but the members also have to match the members of the customer's buying centre at a personal level.

9.3 Team Members and Their Roles

Comprising the team will – ideally – meet a number of criteria, all aimed at matching the individual customer to the outmost extent. In general terms, this requires that the team members – as a whole – can live up to the following:

- Insights concerning products/services, the sales strategy for the customer, the customer and the customer's organisation, and – of course – the other team members
- Relationships – to the customer and to the other team members
- Closeness – in a physical sense
- Available resources – i.e. not limited by other tasks
- Acknowledged and credible – either as an expert or at least as a competent team member
- Will have a "counterpart" in the customer's organisation
- Are motivated – to participate and help
- Can communicate – have the pedagogical skills and know sales methodologies well enough to uncover the customer's business pains and sell/present possible solutions.

The list is hardly exhaustive, but should provide the impression, that a team is not just a team – i.e it is not just a gathering of the – by the point in time – available resources and individuals in the organisation. The members of the team should be selected with great caution and care – in order to balance the interests of the supplying organisation and the aim of matching the customers to the highest degree possible. This is, of course, not always a problem or a root to conflict.

The sales team can also be called a *sales centre* – as a parallel to the customer's *buying centre*, but will often be more organised – at least formally – than the buying centre.

There will be various roles in the sales centre – in the large sales teams, these roles may rest with individuals, while several roles might be handled by the same individual in smaller teams. We have identified eight roles in the sales centre, see figure 9-2.

Strategic responsible/Owner
The team owner is responsible for the team and its activities.

| Strategic reponsible/ Owner | Projekt manager | Hunter/ Scout | Salesman | Specialist/ Expert | Power player | Finance/ Controller | Athoriser/ Approver | Back-office |

Figure 9-2: The sales centre and the roles

The team owner will often have titles as either key account manager, sales director, sales manager or more customer-oriented titles such as customer business development manager, business unit manager, client business development manager, or the like.

The most important element in this role is the commitment and support from the top management. This will be especially important if and when prioritisation of resources is called for.

This role also has the responsibility for the development of the relationship over time and must not only manage the relationship to the customer, but must also manage all relevant internal relationships – i.e. in this role, the key account manager can no longer be successful as a "lone wolf". Being a team leader necessarily also calls for management skills.

From the customer's point of view, this will be the person responsible for the relationship and the collaboration, but not necessarily the person handling all the sales tasks – most of these will be handled by the role of the salesman/scout.

Project manager
The role as project manager is implicitly a part of almost all sales processes, but is typically only formalised in relation to large sales or long sales cycles. The primary responsibility of this role is to ensure constant progress in the sales process – implying that the individual is both capable of foreseeing what is going to happen/should happen and to keep an eye on ongoing activities.

The "foreseeing" part is ensured by process description for the sales process; a "master plan" to describe the desired path for the sales process – including activities and their preferred sequence.

Therefore, this role is required to be staffed with an individual who is able to communicate clearly and consistently, can motivate the other team members to see why constant progress is important and how they may contribute to this.

In many organisations, the role as strategic responsible/ owner and the role as project manager is combined into one – the key account manager.

Salesman/Scout

The role as salesman/scout may be divided into two quite different roles. The salesman role is selling to the customer by identifying sales opportunities and going for them, whereas the scout is the role of identifying potential opportunities and presenting these to members of the buying centre for further discussion.

When the relationship to the customer is fully mature and developed, all members of the team may act as scouts – and it is often seen, that the technical specialists/experts are very well suited for this task.

To detect potential opportunities requires ongoing training – partly to detect the opportunities (also outside the area in which the individual team member is an expert) and partly to participate in peer-to-peer conversations with members of the buying centre to identify and suggest new solutions, i.e. new sales opportunities.

If the members of the team are going to handle the role as scouts, it implies that they have a wide and deep insight into the supplier's products/services and a comparable insight into the customer's business and processes. It also implies that the individual is comfortable with being alone and/or a member of the team – depending on the situation at hand.

Specialist/Expert

This role will provide value to the supplier-customer relationship in two ways – firstly, as the credible expert providing knowhow and competence within his/her specific field of expertise – and secondly, as the provider of a variety of possible solutions to a specific challenge showing the customer that there is more than one way in which to add value to the customer's business. The last type of value contribution may also create a form of "mutual respect" between the expert and the relevant member of the customer's buying centre as the dialogue is about more than solving the challenge in just one way; it is just as much a dialogue concerning the potential of other solutions and opportunities.

The role is therefore very important and is widely used in the IT sector as a number of concrete solutions may only be delivered and implemented when and if the supplier and customer have engaged in a number of exchanges, encompassing questions, discussions and answers. It is, however, not merely a question of mutual respect for knowhow and expertise, it is also a question of mutual personal respect and confidence.

As a specialist you therefore also have to have good communications skills, which implies that although the person is highly respected as a specialist in his/her field, this will not be sufficient if the person has to be a valuable member in the sales centre.

Power player
The power player is important if and when an extraordinary need for additional resources occur, or to break internal principles, or merely to have a top management commitment and participation if new priorities have to be made. The power player therefore has a very important function in the supplier's organisation.

That might also be the case vis-à-vis the customer's buying centre – especially the decision maker and/or approver.

A power player will typically be part of the formal executive management of the corporation, and will have formal authority to make things happen. As hinted before, this may be relevant in terms of internal matters as well as matters directly concerning the supplier-customer relationship. Related to the customer, the power player may be called upon if negotiations are curled up and a set of "fresh eyes" are needed in order to uncurl the situation.

From the team members' point of view, it is absolutely vital that the power player is included in the team's decisions and strategy from the very beginning in order to ensure that the power player knows and understands what is expected of him/her and of the role itself. If this is not the case, the power player may – even unwillingly – undermine the authority of the roles as strategic responsible and/or project manager.

Therefore; use the power player with caution – then he/she will keep the value, internally as well as externally. Last but not least, the team calls the power player in when needed, not when the power player feels inclined to join the team.

Finance/Controller

Financial responsibility or the role as controller may involve several tasks. One central task is to ensure that the investment in the specific supplier-customer relationship pays off – for the customer as well as for the supplier. Thus, it is relevant to implement and execute after-calculations concerning all deliveries to the customer, ensure an ongoing registration of costs associated with the exchanges between the supplier and the customer, and to register and provide a customer profit & loss statement.

This is where there should be a clear link to the discussion about "return on customer relationships" in the supplier's organisation – and by the way, a discussion about "return on supplier relationship" from the customer's point of view.

Authoriser/Approver

The role as authoriser/approver may not be linked directly to the top management, but may be an internal function, which has the final power to decide what is within the capabilities and competences of the corporation and what is not. This is typically installed in an organisation in order to ensure that although the customer's interests are important, the quest to serve the customer should not damage the supplying organisation itself.

Therefore, the sales team must include the authoriser/approver during the sales process in order to align opportunities and capabilities.

Respecting the internal functions and their needs often improves the overall performance of the supplying organisation, but in some instances, the internal functions are more powerful that the sales teams, which may impede the supplier-customer relationship quite considerably.

By formalising the authoriser/approver's relationship to the sales centre, it is possible for the sales team to provide the customer with more realistic projections and forecasts – which, in the end, will prove to be very valuable.

Back-office/Sales support
An often overlooked group of individuals that in reality can make or break the relationship as they are the "hands and feet" of the organisation. Often they are not considered members of the sales team as they serve all customers and all employees of the supplier's organisation. However, this is exactly where the experienced sales team knows that internal relationships may be very valuable – especially if resources are scarce.

9.4 Team Selling or Not – the Checklist

Team selling is – as it is described above – a method to ensure that the relevant and necessary resources are available and prioritised vis-à-vis the specific customer. The team may further be strengthened by adding a role as secretary and a role as an internal process consultant. The first is to ensure documentation of all activities and decisions made; the latter is to ensure that the team actually develops as a team and not just as a group of individuals.

Furthermore, it is a question of how many persons are involved in the exchange with the customer – from the product/service is produced and until it is consumed/used and to what extent these contacts and exchanges are to be regarded as an integrated part of the product/service.

The Relationship Between Buying and Selling

The relationship between a buyer and a seller has been of academic interest over the past years and the academic contribution to understanding the buying behaviour has pointed towards the exchange as the key driver – i.e. all types of exchange from products/services, payments, negotiations, meetings, social events, exhibitions, joint prototype testing etc., etc.

Some compare the development of a supplier-customer relationship to what happens in a relationship between two people, i.e. the development may be described in terms of a number of stages.

The first stage may be characterised as a flirt, during which a mutual acknowledgement of the other part's existence will arise and mutual sympathy may develop. If the sympathy is sufficient, the first exchange may take place – often in the shape of a test order. If the order is fulfilled timely and correctly, the third stage may develop into a more steady relationship – sometimes referred to as marriage. During the fourth stage, mutual knowledge and insights may develop into a level at which the supplier and customer begin to trust one another. The strength of the relationship will then be tested if alternative suppliers or alternative customers show up in the market – such occasions are often used to evaluate and/or re-evaluate the current relationship. It might be worthwhile to note that such evaluations are not objective – i.e. there is no objective truth to the evaluation process or result.

If the result is that the relationship is not satisfactory, the relationship may break or it will be a chance for both parts to make up again – if the dialogue about the evaluation is brought to the others part's attention.

Switching Costs

Quite often, it is necessary to invest in the relationship if the cost of exchange is to be lowered – these investments will often be regarded as important signals to the other part in the relationship as well as an internal way of communicating that this is an important relationship. This will especially be the case, if the investment is in assets that have no alternative use – also labelled as asset specificity[91]. These investments will be sunk costs in the event of a termination of the specific supplier-customer relationship.

Investing in specific assets will, of course, increase dependency and it will also provide an opportunity for the customer to use this dependency as a means to obtain either lower prices, better terms of credit, higher priority if supplies are scarce etc. However, the dependency is often mutual as the customer will be provided with an exact match to his demand.

The risk of opportunistic behaviour will always be present, but it is also worth noting that not all types of behaviour that appears to be opportunistic may actually be rooted in an opportunistic intent. If the information about why the behaviour changes is available, it may be revealed that it is caused by outside factors – i.e. outside factors to the supplier-customer relationship – such as increased competition for the customer, declining sales, etc.

Studies of how salesmen work in large organisations have been undertaken before[92] and they seem to suggest that salesmen are more focused on acquiring new customers than maintaining and nursing existing relationships. As a result of this study, a proposal was made to make the key account manager the centre of a team having full customer responsibility. Ensuring that the organisational structure supports the supplier-customer relationship may also be regarded as an investment in specific assets as studies have revealed that there may also be a link between customer behaviour and the personality type of the key account manager that will handle the specific customer.

Costs may also arise from uncoordinated exchanges – especially those that occur on the basis of the customer's initiative. They may well be within the range of activities accepted by the sales team, but if they are not registered properly, it may not be possible for the supplier to get a trustworthy impression of where and in which suppler-customer relationships profits are made or lost.

Furthermore, uncoordinated acceptance of customer initiatives may cause harm to the relationship at a later stage if these initiatives are identified and brought to a halt – because they are not part of the agreement of how exchanges take place and/or the process concerning these exchanges.

9.5 The Customer's Value Chain Must be Addressed by the Sales Centre

The days of selling products and/or services to a customer and then leaving it to the customer to get the most out of it are over – strong supplier-customer relationships are built on supplier insights into the customer's business, the processes, and how and where the product and/or service may enhance the customer's business in terms of increased competitive edge, lower costs, faster responses, etc.

To get this kind of insight, the members of the sales team have to know and understand the customer's value chain or value network – i.e. where is value created for the customer's customer, how are costs distributed, where are resources and competencies embedded – inside or outside the customer's organisation, etc.

This will be a unique opportunity to identify inputs and outputs of the various functions and departments in the customer's organisation and to understand the key success factors related to these activities and processes.

Some of the key questions in the sales team will be:

- In which parts – functions/departments/activities/ processes – of the customer's organisation can we (the supplier) enhance the customer's business?
- Which inputs/outputs stem from which function/ department?

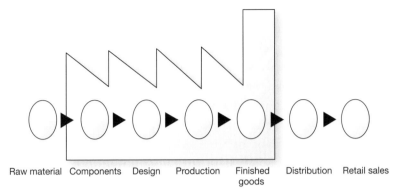

Raw material Components Design Production Finished Distribution Retail sales
goods

Figure 9-3: The customer's value chain/network

- How is value created vis-à-vis other functions/departments in the value chain/network?
- What is the customer's output (to their customers) – and is their market position sufficiently strong?
- How is value created for the customer's customers?
- Where and how may our (the supplier's) product/service make a difference?
- Do we agree on this in the sales team?
- Does the customer agree?
- How can the sales team optimise the customer's use/utilisation of the deliveries, resources and competencies that the sales team represents?
- Who in the team are to handle what members of the customer's buying centre?

Social Competence in the Sales Centre

If a team is to be successful, it has to be able to collaborate internally – coupled with good customer and industry insights. However, teams also mean that the members become interdependent – i.e. individual autonomy and the individual salesman's "ownership" in relation to a customer is history.

The role as team owner therefore also implies teaching the team members to collaborate and nurture attitudes towards sharing of information and acknowledging that all members of the team contribute and are important to the common task, i.e. ensuring the ongoing development of the specific supplier-customer relationship. As mentioned before, a group of individuals working together towards a common goal is not automatically the same as a team.

At the strategic level, the lone rider salesman is out of business. The demands made on businesses are that everything has to be faster, better, higher, etc. – just like the increased demands in sports must be fulfilled if you want to win. The ability to work together with others and to like this common performance and reaching common goals is the key to success for the sales centre. Therefore, teambuilding and team spirit will be underlined in the following as this is not common in most sales organisations where individual performance and success often prevail.

A well-managed key account management team will often be characterised by:

- Common goals and success criteria
- Mutual engagement and trust
- It grows and develops as it meets challenges
- It can handle conflicts even in high-pressure situations
- It is balanced
- Every member knows his/her role in the team.

Team spirit and teamwork are key words as the goal is to reach common goals. Reaching this/these common goal(s) must be a result of the participation of all team members – otherwise some members may not be needed!

In practice, members of a sales centre are often selected according to "what is possible" and not necessarily "what is desirable". This may work out fine, especially if the team management constantly keeps this in mind and monitors the need for supplementary resources.

"Teamwork is the ability to work together towards a common vision"

Closeness to the Customer is Also a Competence

Professional expertise may not solely be the only required competence in the sales centre. Accessibility, language skills, geographical closeness, willingness to assist etc. may be decisive competencies – adding value to the team itself and/or to the customer as a whole or the individuals in the customer's organisation. A few examples may illustrate this:

- In some relationships, it is necessary for the supplier to educate individuals in the customer's organisation – however, this education must be neutral, otherwise it will end up harming the relationship rather than enhancing it
- Accessibility is not just a question of being able to reach members of the sales centre, but it can also be that a "hotline" has been developed to ensure that no matter how large the issue at hand is, there will always be a "back door" to the sales centre responsible in the supplier's organisation
- In some franchise organisations, the insights into how a franchisee unit will develop – possessed by the franchiser – will ensure that the franchisee makes the right decisions as the business develops in the long term.

9.6 Key Account Management is Not Traditional Management

Being the leader of a sales centre is a management task quite unlike any other management task as it involves internally and externally based individuals, i.e. in the supplier's and the customer's organisation. To handle this complex task, a number of disciplines must be mastered:

- Ability to be the People Manager, with strong focus on motivation based on his/her own personality and personal competencies, rather than being the expert on products, services, processes, or procedures. Furthermore, this will often take place in a multi-cultural and multi-professional context

- Ability to think strategically – in terms of one's own organisation and in terms of the customer's organisation. This requires the ability to think short-term and long-term – simultaneously! – in order to ensure continuous progress and achievements
- Coordination, organisation and planning of the team's efforts and resource allocation related to the focus on progress and achievement of results
- Training and coaching of colleagues and own management – potentially also in the customer's organisation
- Ability to communicate own goals and team vision and, furthermore, ability to handle conflicts – internally amongst team members and conflicts related to the supplier-customer relationship and exchange.

At the same time, it has to be a person who can match the individual members of the customer's buying centre and/or organisation. This implies that the key account manager can – and wants to – engage in a dialogue with the customer's top management concerning strategic issues and probably also industry-specific challenges.

Engaging in this kind of dialogue requires credibility – credibility concerning insights into own products, own services and other matters concerning one's own company, but also credibility in terms of competitor insights, collaboration schemes and their consequences, etc. In other words, the dialogue changes from having focus on own superiority to how the customer's business may develop and flourish.

Therefore, the classical key account manager, who masters the company's own products and services, is no longer sufficient.

9.7 Different Types of Teams

As indicated in the introduction to this chapter, a team is not just a team – as we have identified a number of different types of teams.

Teams may be divided in accordance with the following two dimensions:

- Permanent vs. dynamic
- Wide (general) vs. deep (specialized)

Analysing the different types of teams may be helpful when deciding which type is the most appropriate type in the current situation – and also to plan for the team's potential evolvement and change over time if the supplier-customer relationship develops as expected.

	Permanent	Dynamic
Wide	**General, permanent team** Key Accounts	**General, actual team** Identifying relevant competencies
Deep	**Highly specialized, permanent team** Continuous projects for Key Accounts	**Actual, highly specialized team** Project-oriented

Figure 9-4: The four team types

The different types of teams have various focuses and will therefore be relevant for various lengths of time – it should be noted that the different types may have significantly different criteria for measuring success.

The general, permanent team
Static and general teams are often seen in relation to long-lasting relationships between suppliers and their key accounts. Particularly these long relationships – sometimes referred to as partnerships – may benefit tremendously from stable staffing and strong relationships to all relevant functions in the supplier's organisation.

Typically, this sales centre may mirror the buying organisation – and there may even be a match per role vis-à-vis the customer's buying centre. In many of these types of relationships, it is not just professional relationships that develop, more personal relationships also emerge.

Teams like this have a tendency to develop their own subculture – an informal "this is how we do things here", making it easy to work together and to communicate with the customer. Furthermore, the culture will often be so strong that it is quite easy to bring new individuals into the team as they will absorb the culture rather than risking upsetting the relationship, because they will be seen as a "disturbance".

This team type will also be found in companies that establish customer specific departments/offices, with the only purpose of serving that specific customer. Arla Foods is one among many suppliers in the FMCG-industry that has established customer-centric/customer-specific departments to ensure the best possible collaboration with their major key accounts such as ALDI, COOP, etc. Some of these teams have existed for more than a decade and have become a significant contribution to the supplier-customer relationship. The relationship thus contains more than merely professional collaboration. One of the advantages of this has also been to plan for future initiatives, beyond the current planning period, as the daily operations become routine.

Furthermore, it may also be seen as a signal to the customer – regarding their importance – that the supplier is interested in and willing to invest in a permanent and exclusive[93] setup.

A major threat or risk for the collaboration is that the team loses its dynamic capabilities and things become too much of a routine and therefore loses the ability to react or adapt when the relationship is attacked from the outside. The permanent teams may also be costly and they may lack the flexibility allowing the company to utilise its human resources where they may provide the highest impact, due to the focus on consistency in the already established relationships. Finally, there have been some concerns that the emergence of other than merely professional relationships between the individuals could be harmful, but recent observations indicate that these concerns are diminishing on behalf of the search for relationship components that cannot be copied.

The actual, permanent team

This is the permanent team allowing for changes of individuals and also adding or removing competencies. Often relevant when the supplier-customer relationship undergoes changes, e.g. changes from one type of collaboration to another. In some instances, the parties will have agreed that a number of collaboration models have to be tested before choosing the permanent one.

This could e.g. be the case for companies involved in mergers and acquisitions or entering new strategic alliances. Here, new opportunities will constantly arise and it will often be a great opportunity to search for new members of the team in order to see if new collaboration areas can be established.

Flexibility is the name of the game and one of the advantages of this team type is the avoidance of fixed and/or permanent structures, roles and processes. Thus, the resource allocation to the team is constantly monitored and changed when resources are better used elsewhere. Despite this, the customer will rest assured that the relationship has high priority – there would not be a team if this was not the case.

The team can be compared to a "harmonica" as it constantly either expands to encompass more or is compressed to ensure focus.

A drawback of the flexibility and change is that the opportunity for establishing more personal relationships is difficult.

Advantages for this team type are primarily efficiency and focused resource allocation, ensuring fast response and adaptability to changes – whether these are external or internal.

Disadvantages can be the lack of long-term perspectives and the lack of a common subculture. Finally, the managerial challenge is the need for introducing new resources and individuals on an ongoing basis, thereby constantly "stressing" the relationship as new routines and patterns have to be established.

The highly specialized, permanent team

This team is typically used when collaboration is limited and specialised/focused within one or two areas. However, the depth and commitment in the collaboration may be quite substantial. Often it implies that the customer gains access to core resources and competencies in the supplying organisation, i.e. the unique knowhow and insights possessed. This type of collaboration will only be relevant when the supplier stands to gain important experience and/or insights as a result of the collaboration – otherwise it is too narrow. Therefore, it is often seen when the customer is regarded as a "lead-user" or a first mover in the customer's industry.

If research and development is in focus for the company, the highly specialized, permanent team may be seen as a supplement to the general, permanent team – but two teams with very different areas of focus and success. You could say that this type of team is an attempt to add some dynamic capabilities to the general, permanent team.

Disadvantages related to this team type is the use of resources and the lack of flexibility for these, i.e. they may be seen as "locked" to one customer despite their alternative use.

The actual, highly specialized team

The major advantage for this team type is the dynamic capabilities and the ability to constantly change combinations of resources and competencies. Examples of teams of this type may even require the use of external resources – decided jointly by the supplier and customer.

Collaboration of this kind will often be similar to research and development projects as both parties are prepared to follow the path, basically regardless of where it takes them. Especially in industries where "time-to-market" is important, this type of team is valuable as the speed, at which the focus of the collaboration can change, is very high. These teams are often seen as having a higher focus on the professional relationship than on the personal relationship to their counterparts.

Advantages related to this team type are flexibility and the opportunity to optimise the use of resources and competencies in accordance with the interests of the company. Fast responses may also be beneficial if and when the company is involved in frequent product launches. The high focus on professional relationships makes this an easy team to manage.

10. Relationship Marketing Strategy

10.1 Different Theoretical Directions in Relationship Marketing Revisited

In Chapter 1, figure 1-8, we presented and discussed some of the main theoretical contributions to relationship marketing: marketing management, the transaction cost theory, the political-economy paradigm and the network interaction approach. Although illustrative and comprehensive, the different views on relationship marketing do not offer sufficient guidance when it comes to the relationship marketing strategy creation.

The popular marketing management approach, which is the overwhelming contributor to the business school literature in marketing, does not pay much attention to relationships as an essential phenomenon and key dimension in strategy – neither as a part of the marketing process nor as a result of such a process. Marketing management presents itself as a pure analytical, expertise discipline concentrating on the optimisation of resource allocation among different, well-defined customer segments followed by programme formulations vis-à-vis each segment.

In contrast to this, the transaction cost approach gives us a deep holistic understanding of the seller-buyer relationship mechanisms (see Chapters 3 and 4) and what governs them when it comes to the rational economic exchange calculations! Although very useful and applicable as a guidance to gain insight in the distribution of power, risks, benefits and regulating mechanisms in exchanges between two opposing parties, this theory does not orient itself to marketing and hence needs to be connected to other theories.

The two descriptive approaches – political-economy and network-interaction – contribute to the understanding of conflict, co-operation and coalition, both in terms of systems and interactive processes (see Chapter 5, figure 5-3) in 1:1 relationships. They also emphasise patterns of behaviour rather than conscious strategic direction and strategic content.

So, our search for robust relationship marketing concepts and formulas coherently rooted in theoretical relationship marketing approaches as the ones mentioned above does not provide enough good answers to the question: "What theoretical anchor should a marketer then rely on in his or her creation of and reflection on relationship marketing opportunities – whether offensive moves or defensive consolidation?"

10.2 Approaches to Strategy and Relationships

The discussion of relationship marketing strategy has a natural and strong interface to strategy as a research discipline. Like strategy, relationship marketing frameworks are essential – if not derivatives of, then at least strongly inspired by sciences such as economics, political science and sociology in various combinations. So, if the relationship marketing schools do not allow us to develop a clear picture of relationship strategy as a construct, can we then find good answers regarding relationship marketing strategy in the strategy literature? Can we possibly extrapolate? Or is strategy as research discipline as diverse, contradicting, "implicit" and hence confusing concerning relationships as are the relationship marketing schools themselves?

We will summarize the most influential strategy schools[94] with the purpose of building relationship strategies in conceptual alignment with basic assumptions and philosophies of these theories.

The strategy schools indeed differ. Some are mutually ex-

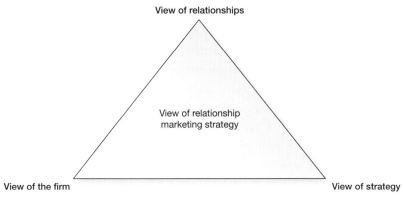

Figure 10-1: The strategic triangle and relationships

clusive. The schools do not represent an evolutionary line in time and sophistication either. And for sure, strategy, marketing and the interplay with the relationship dimension are by far easy to synthesise.

One reason for the diverse perception of strategy and of relationship marketing strategy as a managerial roadmap can be illustrated as shown in figure 10-1.

The strategy schools are rooted in widely different views of what a company is and what strategy is and why. There is a huge mental distance between the perception of the company as rational single-minded, strategy-managed entity and the company as a completely constrained, reactive biological organism. Some of the theories are *prescriptive* and assume strategy to be a superior directive instrument controlled by a master-analytical brainpower, whereas other theories and schools are *descriptive* and concentrating on observation and interpretation, where patterns, structures and beliefs are determinative and not a strategic mastermind at the top of the organisation.

What about relationship marketing strategy in this context, then? Despite the differences in ideas and perceptions of the company and of strategy, all the strategy schools do seek to explain the interfaces, interactions and exchanges between the company and the world surrounding it – customers are given high priority. Just think of the widespread and popular

SWOT as mirror, profile and detector of the company in the world surrounding it! Some schools narrow the scope. Some deal more with the internal life of organisations. But none of the theories of strategy considers the company to exist in a vacuum or in a completely static environment. Strategy unrelated to the interwoven, complex and dynamic interaction between the "inside" and the "outside" makes no sense.

It is a striking paradox that the relationship views of the many strategic schools – and hence also their contributions to the learning and thinking of relationship marketing – have to be extracted from them. Relationships are not framed into the strategy theories explicitly as objects, although important underneath and integrated in each of the strategy stories – be it as preambles, driving forces, success factors, variables, influents, exchange systems, networks – or results.

We have extracted a schematic, simplified representation of some of the strategy schools and their underlying builtin relationship logics and meanings. Not all features are included in the overview, but some main conclusions become apparent:

Four strategy schools are included: Positioning, cultural pattern, entrepreneurship and configuration. The more or less opposing propositions, assumptions and views of the different strategy schools are described in figure 10-2 as single, comparable statements and one-liners.

We have then deducted what each strategy school would eventually have to say about customers, the relationship view and relationship marketing strategy. These findings are derivatives, implications and interpretations of the schools and not explicit conclusions drawn by the scholars of each direction.

Figure 10-2 illustrates some of the variety and even profound differences in the strategy literature between the proponents of the schools. Exactly the same kind of divergent perceptions and ideas are "transferred" to the study of customer relations and to the guiding principles for marketing strategy in a relationship context.

Some rather sharp lines dividing the strategy regimes as

	Strategy as:			
	Positioning	Cultural pattern	Entrepreneurship	Configuration
Authors	Porter	Barney	Afuah	Chan and Mauborgne
View of the company	Strategy before structure	Structure before strategy	Vision before all	Strategy as disrupt organic change
View of strategy	Normative. Content calculation	Descriptive. Collective process	Descriptive. Individual process	Normative. Paradigm alignment
Message	Only a few generic strategies available and desirable	Core competencies applicable in various markets	Envisioning leader creator of perspective	Transitions through quantum leaps followed by integration
Perspective	Outside-in Opportunity/threats	Inside-out Strength/weaknesses	Outside-in Opportunity/threats	Integrated outside-in and inside-out
Strategy skill	Analytical centralized	Behavioural decentralized	Intuitive individualistic	Episodic responsive
Customer view	Obtain dominance. Simple exchange view	Create mutual benefits. Complex exchange view	View customer as opportunity source. Diffusion of innovation view	Synchronise with configuration. Life cycle integrative view
Relationships as	Mobility Barriers. Relationship economics	Unique Resources. Organisational economics	Concept attributes. Innovation economics	Categorical characteristics. Archetype economics
Relationship marketing strategy as	Generic relationship strategy	Incremental, interactive behaviour	Emergent or disruptive value chain innovation	Categorically aligned archetype configuration

Figure 10-2: Strategy schools and relationship marketing strategies

presented here leap to the eye, e.g. "Strategy and hence relationship marketing strategy is an analytically based discipline which can lead to organisational direction and specific recommendations – like the classic marketing by the way", versus: "Strategy is not a top down rational masterminded calculation, but a complex decentralised accumulation of learning, interaction and resource accumulation which ultimately allows the company to act and adapt. The inside of organisations is what counts". Hence also, some rather different perceptions of relationships arise: Relations as *mobility barriers* as opposed to relations as *unique resources* and/or relations as concept attributes versus relations as categorical characteristics of a specific company configuration and structure (cf.

Chapter 8.2 – the Miles and Snow typology). So, what relationship marketing strategy really is….depends!

In figure 10-2, we have presumed to attach a genuine business economic rationale to each of the strategy schools. The term relationship economics corresponds to the rationales presented earlier in Chapter 3. Organisational economics mean considerations concerning resource value creation in a total and complex sense – which include customer relations. The entrepreneurial approach relies on innovation economics – will it fly? Under this regime we treat relations partly as a part of the business idea itself (Dell direct as opposed to Digital indirect) and also external relations as a part of the entrepreneurial organisation (entrepreneurs have ambitions of reaching far beyond the resource base they control). Archetype economics is, as we see it, spun into the individual approach to customer relationships, which company configurations lead to. Prospectors and defenders (Chapter 8) have definitely different practises and focus areas in their customer interfaces.

These business economic distinctions and labels are fakes in the sense that not all the strategy schools they are aligned to are rooted in economics and "rational man thinking". Some are descriptive, system-oriented, some based on social sciences, Darwinism etc. Despite this scientific alchemy, we find is useful to highlight the business economic aspect of each school serving us as the intellectual bridge to a relationship marketing discussion.

So, four different propositions of relationship marketing strategy are now on the table:

Positioning
The prescriptive generic strategy proposition (Porter) for creating sustainable competitive advantage in a new dress where the strategy formula jumps out of a relationship perspective and a relationship-economic calculation with focus on opportunities and threats rather than strengths and weaknesses.

Cultural pattern

According to which relationship marketing strategy can be observed, described and interpreted as an element of the organisation's pool of unique resources and hence – possibly – a core competence. This core competence is expressed as the company's interactive relationship behaviour and hence its portfolio of customer relationships being strategic assets. Interactive behaviour leading to resource strength and superiority assumes a mutual beneficial attitude towards customers relying on a complex, partly unmanageable exchange view. Focus on SW and not OT.

Entrepreneurship

Disruptive entrepreneurial innovations very often consist of a destructing or remodelling of value chains and/or new offerings with a remarkable reformulated customer-concept relationship (IKEA, Timex, SecondLife). Here relationship marketing strategy is embedded in the vision and the opportunity-driven features of a genuine business idea. We call it emergent or disruptive value chain innovation.

Configuration

Configuration means organic change – often revolutionary – to comply with environmental transformation (Intel from memory chip units to microprocessors) in inflicting moments. In order to compete – i.e. fulfil its role in the business eco system, companies must keep up with the archetype configuration it has "chosen" – be it proactive or reactive, offensive or defensive. Relationships follow the characteristics of the archetype category. In most periods, relationships play an integrative role ensuring that the archetype of the company is kept vital. Relationship marketing strategy should allow the company to both ensure configuration-environment synchronisations and the grasping of changes, when a remapping is necessary.

Only the positioning school is technique and methodology-oriented. It offers a basket of analytical tools and sequences to the marketer. Not to say that the positioning school is neither more "right" than the others or represents the highest level of sophistication in an evolutionary sense. The other schools simply do not give specific answers to concrete business questions such as: "How do I as a manager, specialist or consultant attack my relationship marketing strategy?

Let us take a closer look at each of the relationship marketing schools.

10.3 Relationship Marketing Strategy as Positioning

The positioning school assumes that the market place is a battle field. The powerful ones decide and the winner takes it all. Sustainable competitive advantage is a dominance game. Only a few positions in each industry are attractive. They are named generic strategies. Decision-making is centralised. Organisations obey and execute. Strategic thinking is an expert discipline.

According to the positioning school – why is it that some companies succeed in creating a high and outstanding level of customer loyalty through a relationship-based generic strategy – and gain above average profits through dominance, while others do not?

In economic terms, the idea of the *extra customer relationship profitability* is a reflection of different streams of direct and indirect contributions generated at the transactional level of the relationship. This generates higher prices, larger volumes, lower costs of servicing the customer, lower defection rates, reduced sales- and marketing expenses, increased buying frequency etc. What the company must sometimes do, in order to maximise relationship economy, i.e. the relationship-generated plus-revenue streams, is to undertake investments in customisation of assets. Companies are sometimes reluctant to do so due to possible asset redeployment losses and hence dependence and vulnerability in terms of loss of bargaining power.

When customers tend to rebuy and behave as loyalists over a longer period of time and when this behaviour contributes to the financial success of the supplier, it can to some extent be explained by a similar relationship-economic logic at the customer side. Depending on the category of product or service and the fit within the regulating mechanisms, a customer gets more value for "loyalty money" in the sense that the perceived marginal transaction costs going through an extended purchasing process exceed the expected benefit that such a process could possibly generate.

Therefore, the main suggestion is that it may pay off for the customer to demonstrate loyalty from an economic, technical or psychological standpoint. This, however, may sometimes be modified by the overall strategic approach pursued by the organisation in question. Relationship-oriented buying adds more net value to the buyer than control and autonomy in combination with somewhat higher transaction costs could alternatively lead to.

If above average profitability assumes high loyalty, and if such strong loyalty requires extraordinary customer satisfaction, then the crucial strategic question in conjunction with customer relationships according to the positioning school is not "how do we obtain and retain satisfied customers?", but instead "how do we develop *extremely* satisfied customers?" Successful strategic development founded on a customer relationship strategy means creating extraordinary benefits not just sufficient ones. Why? Because outstanding performance separating the company from the crowd depends on the "last step on the ladder" bridging the gap between satisfied and extremely satisfied customers[95], as illustrated in figure 10-3, creating a mobility barrier.

It should be noted that "satisfaction" must be dealt with in a relative sense, i.e. relative to expectations and competitors. In addition to this, some companies may find that marginal investments in customer services and loyalty programmes are less attractive than investments in the core product.

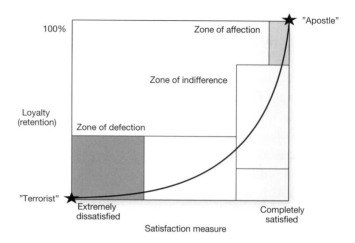

Figure 10-3: A satisfied customer is loyal. Source: Heskett, Jones, Loveman, Sasser and Schlesinger (1994)

There are important modifications to the above rationale that customer satisfaction sustains loyalty:

According to Storbacka:[96] Customer loyalty is not always based on a positive attitude as such, and long-term relationships do not necessarily require positive commitment from the customers. The distinction is important because it challenges the idea that customer satisfaction (attitudinal dimension) leads to long-lasting relationships (behavioural dimension).

So, the simple notion that customer satisfaction leads to customer retention, which in turn leads to profitability, might be too simplistic and possibly misleading to many businesses. Intuitively, while the goal of increased customer satisfaction might prove productive, it might as well increase expectations and almost by definition lead to increased dissatisfaction rates. When you decrease your expectation, you increase your chance of happiness.

The idea of creating extraordinary customer satisfaction as the prime loyalty source should always be calculated along with the marginal contribution it can provide and the costs of an increased expectation level. Our rationale must therefore be perceived in relation to competitors and in relation to alternatives.

Combining *"positioning where"* – niche versus total market – with *"positioning how"* – cost or quality – now enables us to orchestrate a new typology for understanding relationship marketing strategies in accordance with the positioning school. Not surprisingly, we have named this typology Generic relationship marketing strategies (see figure 10-4). The label – *generic* – underlines the fact that the strategies are genuine and bound together in a system of mutual business economic logic and that sustainable competitive advantage depends on different and distinct sources.

Transaction cost leadership means that a company acquires sustainable and decisive relationship economic advantages within the total market. Such transaction cost advantages over competitors lead to higher profitability. A very loyal and extremely satisfied customer portfolio will, among other advantages, result in considerably lower sales and marketing costs.

Figure 10-4: Four generic relationship marketing strategies

Although it is the relative transaction cost position of the company that generates the above average financial performance and hence the sustainable advantage, the other side of the transaction cost leadership coin is about the advantages that the customers receive. The low perceived transaction cost level in terms of extraordinary security, standardisation, reutilisation, optimised regulating mechanisms and so forth, becomes the heart of the relationship incentive for the customer, whereas the loyalty from the customer is the reward that the transaction cost leader receives.

Differential-based relationship advantages can be a successful strategy for companies aiming at market leadership. A *relationship differentiator* addresses the market as a whole, either with a highly *standardised* concept through attributes like convenience, simplicity, productivity, comfort etc., or with *mass customisation,* such as e.g. the eyeglass industry. Relationship differentiators harvest extra profits on a quality-generated loyalty that can be translated into higher prices, lower marketing and service expenses or extension and prolongation of the customer life cycles.

Differentiation advantages in the relationship sense can either stem from structural strategic moves at critical points in the industry life cycle, such as discount stores in the mature retail market, or by early adaptation to emerging market needs.

In addition to the generic relationship strategies targeting the total market, substantial competitive advantages by conquering one of the attractive positions can instead be obtained by focusing on specific relationship segments which possess a preference for certain relationship attributes. By *quality segment specialisation,* a company decides to specify its assets and competencies to well-defined segments or individual customers, leaving the rest of the market out of scope. The more distinct the more attractive and accessible special relationship segments are, the higher the likelihood of success within a quality segment. Specialisation does imply that a company specifies its products to suit certain target groups or even individual customers with the purpose of fulfilling relationship needs better than competitors or substitutes. The suppliers attract customers who are not completely satisfied with the relationship offerings from cost leaders or differentiators and increase their switching costs through a relationship quality offering.

A *transaction cost niche player* is focused on selected customer segments that demand very specific relationship-economic advantages. It could be access, self-service, transparency, reversibility, special kinds of deliveries etc.

Each of the four generic relationship strategies highlights distinct pathways to increased loyalty and hence outstanding performance. Relationship economy and relationship quality represent two such distinctly different directions where clear positioning and unique competencies support each other.

The principles behind the positioning school and relationship economy are very similar. According to the positioning school, strategy is content-centric and relationship strategies rely on specific customer-supplier loyalty logic.

10.4 Customer Relationships as a Strategic Resource

If customer relationships, e.g. measured as market share, are *not* positions or an outcome of positioning in terms of a smart business strategy often first moving, what are they then? The cultural school of strategy rejects the outside-in way of creating strategy and the idea suggesting the existence of a few predefined, winning positions. This school views positions (products, brands, businesses, portfolios etc.) to be just a snapshot of what a bundle of dynamic capabilities have created – right now. Capabilities and competencies is what create winners, whereas concrete positions change over time – sometimes rapidly. So, strategy is perspective and value-driven patterns of organisational behaviour. Strategy is a collective process. Perspective overrules direction. Resources and competencies are by nature internal, more or less valuable and not just available on the factor market. They are complex, invisible and process drivers in a sensitive cultural context.

Competencies that will enable a company to develop, maintain and renew customer relationship strengths across markets, long-term and superior to competitors, will make such a company prosper. Capabilities that really make a difference must be relevant, valuable, rare, inimitable and not substitutable. In short: unique.

A cultural-based approach to relationship marketing strategy means to acquire a deep understanding of:

- The nature of customer relationships as strategic assets
- The specific capabilities required to obtain the customer relationships' superiority
- Insight in the process of acquiring, concentrating, accumulating, complementing, conserving and recovering competencies of crucial importance for relationship strengthening.

Do not misinterpret the cultural school. Although there is no attempt to design "how-to models", toolboxes, analytical concepts etc., it does not disregard market forces, competition, the need to pitch for market shares and market leadership. But it would perceive relationship marketing strategy and the advantages of such strategy as an outcome of long-term behavioural norms and not of a particular position. The resource-based view on relationships recognises the existence of an inseparable link between "image" and culture with culture as the driver.

10.5 Entrepreneurial Strategy and Customer Relationships

The entrepreneurial school is neither focused on position-dominance as such nor on core competence development and dynamic capabilities. Strategic thinking, according to the entrepreneurial school, is vision – "seeing" before it becomes obvious. Intuition as the forerunner of analysis.

The entrepreneurial approach to strategy focuses on the ongoing search for new opportunities, which are not apparent to established players in the market.

The customer relationship aspect plays an important role for the entrepreneurial company in its conceptualisation of the vision to a business idea and also at the early stages of the life of the new enterprise:

- Customer relationships as conceptualisation of the vision to a business idea
  · The business idea is a customer relationship innovation
  · The business idea is a value chain innovation
- The role of the customer relation at the early stages of the new enterprise
  · Customers are a learning lab
  · Customer relationships contribute as proof of concept, references and chasm-crossers
  · Customer relationships as take-off of an epidemic effect in the diffusion of innovation
  · Relations and networks as hierarchy stretching

The vast majority of new businesses can be labelled market innovations as opposed to technology innovations. Among the market innovations, value propositions based on innovative customer relationship thinking are far from rare. When IKEA offers its customers a series of experiences during their visits in the stores and the satisfaction of having built their own furniture at home, it is a deliberate relationship innovation of the core value proposition. In the entrepreneurial sense, customer relationships can be treated as a source of business opportunity and customer relationship strategy as a question of innovative product definition.

Value chains tend to become reinforcing and much innovation strengthens and complements effective value chain structures, prolonging their lives and protecting capital investments and other assets adapted to a certain system or paradigm. The stronger and the longer a value chain protects and supports itself through innovation and adoption, the greater the latent entrepreneurial opportunities will be. So, if we consider supplier-customer relationships to be a sub-chain of the overall value chain, then entrepreneurial thinking and reformulation of this relation can be disrupted and ultimately lead to destruction. The entrepreneurial message with respect to relationship marketing strategy is to look for successful, mature "relationship chains" that can be shaken. Sir Richard Branson has named them "Up against fat cats".

Customer relations are crucial to the entrepreneurial company and, in most cases, a key to survival at the early stages. Customers are learning labs, where the entrepreneur can observe, analyse, change and experiment. Listen. Ask questions. Simulate alternatives. Without close and committed customer relationships in the pre-launch phases, many entrepreneurs will fail. Not only are customers a test lab, they are also risk-reducing stakeholders for the entrepreneurial initiative.

Also, customer references of the right kind can act as an invaluable leverage, when the young company meets the market. Hence, early, prestige references can open the doors to the market: "If NASA can use it, well…."

Customer relationships in an entrepreneurial perspective is not just a question of meeting the market pre-launch to learn the most and reduce later customer acceptance the most. It is also a question of initiating relations to and acquiring a customer base with innovator characteristics. I.e. customers which can cause the epidemic effect in time, space and segments that make the diffusion of innovation happen. From this perspective, relationship marketing strategy in the entrepreneurial mode becomes a prerequisite for diffusion of innovation.

Innovative entrepreneurs have ambitions far exceeding the resources they control. They face a structural resource gap between goals and means. One way of overcoming the gap is to extend or stretch the entrepreneurial organisation by building strong networks with prospective customers and other potential stakeholders. Hence, successful entrepreneurial thinking is not only vision-centric, but also relationship-centric!

10.6 The Integrative Configuration View on Marketing Strategy and Relationships

According to the configuration school, a company experiences a few periods of dramatic change, shake-ups or bumps, requiring total adaption to new environmental conditions – and long periods of stability with introvert focus. So, the risk of episodic, radical change and the necessity of consistent, continued supportive integration processes are two conflicting forces to be taken care of by the strategists at the same time. Relationship marketing strategy is basically a question of alignment between the company as an organism and the environment governed and constrained by the stereotype. Companies stick to paradigms and processes are archetype-specific. Archetypes dictate the roles and nature of relationships.

In order to succeed, companies must synchronise with the environment. Companies must allow relationships to emerge, but should also hold the view of relationships as deliberate constructions. The dilemma between the spontaneity of emergent relationship behaviour and the determined category behaviour reflects the trade-off between the need for archetype reinforcement and paradigm challenge.

As a mirror of the view of the company as a responsive-integrative organism, customer relations in the configuration perspective pass through the stages of emergence, development, stability, adaption, struggle and revolution. The customer relationship life cycle perspective is driven by the company's need to destroy and integrate relationships as paradigms lose their explanatory power. Customer relationships are both a resource ensuring synchronisation and a position in the sense that a certain archetype behaviour finds and occupies its niche. Hence, the configuration school combines the outside-in with the inside-out perspective.

The configuration school does not assume that only a few positions are attractive in terms of generic strategies. Neither does it prescribe a few performance-superior relationship behaviour patterns. What it does is to underline the organisational and hence the customer relationship eco-cycle as a perpetual force that could and should be converted into relationship programmes. This idea is illustrated in figure 10-5.

Figure 10-5 distinguishes between the periods of integration and control (rational, constrained, struggling relationships) and eras of episodic confusion leading to crisis, confusion and revitalisation through creativity and "skunk". Figure 10-5 illustrates that customer relationship strategy changes during the cycle from a maintaining via an adopting to an experimenting behaviour.

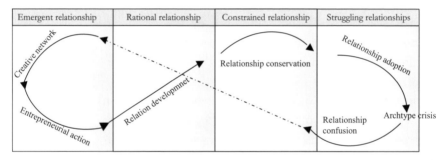

Figure 10-5: Customer relations as a modified eco-cycle. Source: Hougaard & Bjerre

Our finding is that none of the strategy schools are anchored in relationship thinking. It is, nevertheless, possible to apply their internal rationales and basic principles to a relationship-based view, which we have done. It is interesting to see how much the strategic schools differ in their approaches. Hence, it is equally difficult to present firm conclusions on relationship strategy.

Notes

Preface

[a]   Evans and Wurster (2000).

Chapter 1

[1]   Grönroos (1990; 1992), Morgan and Hunt (1994), Gummesson (1996).
[2]   Egan (2001).
[3]   See note 2.
[4]   Levitt (1960).
[5]   Børge Olsen – the founder of the Danish retail chain IRMA.
[6]   Hedaa (1991).
[7]   One important aspect of the relationship marketing definition requires attention. The seeming philanthropy of the altruistic sentiments implied by relationship marketing (mutuality, equality…) might seem to contradict the fact that that profit motive is still being a principal business driver. The difference between relationship marketing and traditional marketing is that relationship marketing to some extent replaces the idea of manipulation with the idea of co-operation, subject though to differences in regulating mechanisms. Terminating relationships that are not profitable is an underlying assumption behind the above definition.
[8]   Payne (1988) e.g. identifies four different research schools within relationship marketing: (1) The Scandinavian School identified by the Swedish School of Economics and Business Administration, (2) The Anglo Australian School, (3) the Northern American School and (4) the

IMP Group (Industrial Marketing and Purchasing Group) based in Sweden.

9 The IMP-school refers to the "Industrial Marketing and Purchasing Group" or "International Marketing and Purchasing Group" – depending on the audience (Ford, 1995, p. 2). See also note 11.

Chapter 2

10 Alderson (1957).

11 Kotler, (1988, p. 8) and as referred to in figure 1-6.

12 Industrial Marketing & Purchasing Group

13 Håkansson and Snehota (1995) and as referred to in figure 1-10.

14 Kotler (1988, p. 9).

15 See figure 1-3 in chapter 1.

16 Bagozzi, (1974, p. 78).

17 In chapter 5, the driving forces of relationships are examined in further detail.

18 This is also referred to as "path dependency". The implication of this is that the future of a relationship will, at least to some extent, be dependent on exchanges in the past, the way conflicts have been resolved etc.

19 Bagozzi (1975, p. 32).

20 Bagozzi (1975, p. 36).

21 We use the term distribution literature to refer to physical distribution of goods and services, as defined by Stern and El-Ansary (1992).

22 Bagozzi (1975).

23 Grönroos (1990).

24 Dwyer, Schurr and Oh (1987) listed four important reasons for focusing on exchange processes in marketing in their article: "Developing Buyer-Seller Relationships" (p. 11):

a) "First, exchange serves as a focal event between two or more parties.

b) Second, exchange provides an important frame of reference for identifying the social network of individuals and institutions that participate in its formation and execution.

c) Third, it affords the opportunity to examine the domain of objects or physic entities that get transferred.

d) Finally, and most important, as a critical event in the marketplace it allows the careful study of antecedent and processes for buyer-seller exchange.

[25] As described by Arndt (1983), as he has refined the work carried out by Stern and Reve (1980) and later supplemented by Skytte (1990).

[26] Arndt (1983, p. 44).

[27] See also chapter 5 for description of driving forces of relations.

[28] Achrol et al. (1983); Arndt (1983).

[29] Pfeffer et al. (1978).

Chapter 3

[30] Williamson (1975; 1985).

[31] Reichheld (1996).

[32] Heikkila (1996).

[33] See also figure 2-3 in chapter 2.

[34] As described in detail in subsection 2.2.

[35] Williamson (1975).

[36] Boston Consulting Group – BCG.

[37] Described as different types in figure 4-1 in chapter 4.

Chapter 4

[38] Kunøe (1994).

[39] Svanholmer (1996).

[40] See also subsection 2.3 on different exchange types.

[41] Barnard and Ehrenberg (1997).

[42] Gummeson (1996).

[43] Kotler (1992).

[44] Svanholmer (1996).

[45] Reichheld (1993; 1996).

[46] Alternative approaches to this is presented in chapter 6, subsection 6.1

[47] Heskett, Jones, Loveman, Sasser and Schlesinger (1994).

[48] Payne et al. Reltionship Marketing

Chapter 6

[49] See subsection on "Strategic Behaviour".

[50] Kurzrock (1996, p. 121).

[51] See also the discussion regarding Aaker (1996) and the loyalty pyramid.

[52] See chapter on "Relationship Economics".

[53] See chapter 8 on "The Individualised Approach to Relationships".

[54] See section on Political Economy Paradigm.

[55] See chapter 2.

[56] Gummesson (1996).

[57] Nonaka and Takeuchi (1995).

Chapter 7

[58] See also chapter 5 on the "Driving forces of Customer Relationships".

[59] Internal and external refers to the concept of the political economy paradigm, i.e. internal and external is related to the dyadic relationship between the organisations in focus.

[60] Hayes, Jenster and Aaby (1996). This section has been taken much further in "Industry Analysis" in Jenster and Hussey (2001).

[61] See subsection on risks related to relationships.

[62] See also chapter 2 introducing the Political Economy Paradigm.

[63] Nelson and Winter (1982).

[64] Penrose (1959).

[65] Williamson (1975), and the customisation of assets.

[66] See also chapter 10 for further details.

[67] See also chapter on driving forces of relationship development.

[68] See also the contribution by Reichheld in figure 9-1.

[69] See also chapter 1.

[70] Sawheney and Parikh (2001).

[71] Reichheld and Schefter (2000).

[72] See chapter 10 on relationship balance system.

Chapter 8

[73] See chapter 2 on the political economy paradigm for reference.

[74] Porter (1980).

[75] Tollin (1990).

[76] Miles and Snow (1978, p. 11).

[77] The three step approach introduced in chapter 7 will be beneficial here.

[78] Miles and Snow (1978).

[79] Miles et al. (1988, p. 529).

[80] Italics added by us.

[81] Miles and Snow (1978, pp. 37-38) and Thompson (1973).

[82] Miles and Snow (1978, p. 56).

[83] Italics added by us.

[84] 1994, The definition of The International Center for Competitive Excellence.

[85] 1998, Martin Christopher's definition.

[86] Krajlik (1983).

[87] Kjeldsen (1997).

[88] Shapiro (1985), Krajlik (1983) and Tanskanen (1994).

[89] Kjeldsen (1997).

Chapter 9

[90] As elaborated on in chapter 8.

[91] According to Oliver Williamsson

[92] Laurids Heedaa.

[93] Exclusive refers to the fact that the focus is solely on the one customer, and that insights gained from this collaboration are not shared with anybody else.

Chapter 10

[94] Mintzberg et alt.

[95] Earl Sasser: "The gulf between satisfied and *completely* satisfied customers can swallow a business".

[96] Storbacka (1994).

References

Aaker, D. (1991) *Managing Brand Equity: Capitalizing on the Value of a Brand Name*, The Free Press.

Aaker, D. (1996) *Building strong brands*, The Free Press.

Achrol, R. S., Reve, T. and Stern, L. W. (1983*) The Environment of marketing Channel Dyads: A Frame Work for Comparative Analysis*, Journal of Marketing, vol. 47 (fall), pp. 55-67.

Ahrnell, B-M. and Nicou, M. (1989) *Kunskapsföretagets marknadsföring – att utveckla förtroende, relationer och kompetens,* Liber.

Alderson, W. (1957) *Marketing behaviour and Executive Action*, Richard D. Irwin

Alonzo, V. (1994) *Till death do us part*, Incentive Marketing.

AMA (1985) *Board Approves New Marketing Definition*, Marketing News.

Arndt J. (1979) *Toward a Concept of Domesticated Markets*, Journal of Marketing.

Arndt, J. (1983) *The Political Economy Paradigm: Foundation for Theory Building in Marketing*, Journal of Marketing, vol. 47 (fall), pp. 44-54.

Arnerup, B. & Edvardson, B. (1992) *Marknadsföring av tjänste,*. Studenterlitteratur.

Bagozzi, R. P. (1974) *Marketing as an Organized Behavioral System of Exchange*, Journal of Marketing, vol. 38, pp. 77-81.

Bagozzi, R. P. (1975) *Marketing as Exchange*, Journal of Marketing, vol. 39, pp. 32-39.

Bagozzi, R. P. (1975) *Marketing as Exchange*, Journal of Marketing, vol. 39, pp. 32-39.

Barnard, N. and Ehrenberg, A. S. C. (1997) *Advertising: Strogly pervasive or nudging?,* Journal of Advertising Research.

Barney, J. B. (1991) *Firm Resources and Sustained Competitive Advantage*, Journal of Management, vol. 17, pp. 99-120.

Berry, L. L. (1983) *Relationship Marketing: Perspectives on Services Marketing*, American Marketing Association.

Berry, L.L. and Parasuramen, A. (1991) *Marketing of Services: Competing through Quality*, Free Press.

Bjerre, M. (1999) *Key Account Management of Complex Strategic Relationships*, Ph.D. dissertation Copenhagen Business Scholl.

Bjerre, M. (1999b) *Key Account Management – et strategisk værktøj*, Børsens Forlag.

Bjerre, M., Ulrich, T. and Refshøj, J. (2008) *Kundefokus skaber konkurrencekraft*, Børsens Forlag.

Blois, K. (1995) *Relationship Marketing – is it always appropriate?*, Management Research Papers.

Blomqvist, R., Dahl, J. and Haeger, T.(1993) *Relationsmarknadsföring – strategier og metoder i Servicekonkurrens*, Göteborg.

Borden, N. H. (1964) *The Concept of the Marketing Mix*, Journal of Advertising Research, vol. June, pp. 2-7.

Brinberg, D. and McGrath, J. E. (1985) *Validity and the Research Process*, Sage Publications.

Carman, J. M. (1980) *Paradigms for Marketing Theory*, Research in Marketing, vol. 3, pp. 1-36.

Christopher, M. (1997) *Marketing Logistics*, Butterworth-Heinemann

Christopher, M. (1998) *Logistics and Supply Chain Management*, Pitman Publishing.

Christopher, M., Payne, A. and Ballantyne, D (1991) *Relationship Marketing*, Butterworth-Heinemann

Christopher, M., Payne, A. and Ballantyne, D (1999) *Relationship Marketing*, Butterworth-Heinemann

Christopher, M., Payne, A. and Ballantyne, D. (1991) *Relationship Marketing for Competitive Advantage – Winning and Keeping Customer*, Butterworth-Heinemann.

Coase, R. (1937) *The Nature of the Firm*, Economica.

Collins, J. C. and Porras, J. I. (1995) *Skabt til succes – visionæ-*

re virksomheders succeskriterier, Børsens Forlag.

Council on Financial Competition (1995) *Perfecting Custo-mer Retention and Recovery – Overview of Economics and Proven Strategies,* Advisory Board.

Cram, T. (1994) *The power of relationship marketing: How to keep the customer for life,* Financial Times.

Cron, W. L. and Levy, M. (1987) *Sales Management Perfor-mance Evaluation: A Residual Income Perspective,* Journal of Personal Selling and Sales Management, vol. August.

Crosby, L.A. and Stephens, N. (1987) *Effects of Relationship Marketing on Satisfaction, Retention and Prices in the Life Insurance Industry,* Journal of Market Research.

Cumberland, F. (1999) *Markedsføring – materialesamling,* Samfundslitteratur.

Cyert, R.M. and March, J.G. (1963) *A Behavioural Theory of the Firm,* Prentice Hall Englewood Cliffs.

Daft, R. L. and Weick, K. E. (1984) *Toward a Model of Or-ganisations as Interpretation Systems,* Academy of Manage-ment Review, vol. 9, No. 2, pp. 284-295.

Dick, A.S. and Kunal, B. (1994) *Customer Loyalty: Toward an integrated Conceptual Framework,* Journal of Academy of Marketing Science.

Dietrich, M. (1994) *Transaction Cost Economics and Beyond,* Routledge.

Doyle, P. (1995) *Marketing in the new millennium,* European Journal of Marketing, vol. 29, pp. 23-41.

Duus, H. J. (1994) *Economic Foundations for an Entrepreneu-rial Marketing Concept,* Handelshøjskolen i København.

Dwyer, F.R., Schurr, P.H. and Oh, S. (1987) *Developing bu-yer-seller relationships,* Journal of Marketing.

Dwyer, R. F., Schurr, P. H. and Oh, S. (1987) *Developing Buyer-Seller Relationships,* Journal of Marketing, vol. 51, pp. 11-27.

Egan, J. (2001) *Relationship Marketing – Exploring relational strategies in marketing,* Pearson Education.

Enis, B. M. and Mokwa, M. P. (1979) *The Marketing Man-agement Matrix: A Taxonomy for Strategy Comprehension,* in Ferrell, O. C., Brown, S. W. and Lamb, C. W. Jr. (eds.), Conceptual and Theoretical Developments in Marketing, Proceedings Series, AMA.

Eriksen, B. (1992) *The Resource-Based Theory of the Firm: A New Paradigm for Strategy Research?*, Management Research Institute, CBS.

Floyd, S. and Wooldridge, R. (1992) *Middle Management involvement in strategy and its association with strategic type*, Strategic Management Journal, Summer Special Issue, vol. 13, pp. 153-167.

Forbrugerstyrelsen, Denmark 2001.10.15

Ford, D. (1980) *The Development of Buyer-Seller Relations in Industrial Markets*, European Journal of Marketing.

Ford, D. (1990) *Understanding Business Markets: Interaction, Relationships and Networks*. Academic Press London.

Ford, D. (1995) *Understanding Business Markets*, International Thomson Business Press.

Ford, D. (ed.) (1995) *Understanding Business Marketing*, Dryden Press

Ford, D., Håkansson, H. and Johanson, J. (1986) *How do companies interact?*, Industrial Marketing and Purchasing.

Fornell, C. (1992) *A National Customer Satisfaction Barometer. The Swedish Experience*, Journal of Marketing.

Foss, N. J. (1993) *Theories of the Firm, Contractual and Competence Perspectives*, Journal of Evolutionary Economics.

Freeman, R. E. (1984) *Strategic Management – a Stakeholder Approach*, Pitman.

Freytag, P. V. (1991) *Leverandørsamarbejde –Koncipering af en referencemodel Bind I og II*, Samfundslitteratur, 1991.

Gordon, I. (1998) *Relationship Marketing*. John Willey & Sons.

Groenewegen, J. (ed) (1996) *GRASP: Conference Report Transaction Cost and Beyond*

Groenewegen, J. (ed.) (1996) *Transaction Cost Economics and Beyond*, Kluwer Academic Publishers.

Grönroos, C. (1990) *Relationship approach to the marketing function in service contexts: the marketing and organization behaviour interface,* Journal of Business Research.

Grönroos, C. (1992) *Facing the challenge of service: The economic of service,* Swedish School of Economics and Business Administration in Helsinki.

Grönroos, C. (1993) *From Marketing Mix to relationship Marketing: Toward a Paradigm Shift in Marketing,* Swedish School of Economics and Business Administration in Helsinki.

Grönroos, C. (1994) *Quo vadis, marketing? Toward a relationship marketing paradigm,* Journal of Marketing Management.

Grönroos, C. (1995) *The Rebirth of Modern Marketing,* Meddelande från svenka Handelshöskolan i Helsinki.

Guiltinan, J. and Paul, G. (1991) *Marketing Management: Strategies and programmes,* McGraw-Hill.

Gummesson, E. (1987) *The new marketing – developing long-term interactive relationships,* Long Range Planning.

Gummesson, E. (1990) *The part-time marketer,* University of Karlstad.

Gummesson, E. (1996) *Relationsmarkedsføring. Fra 4P til 30R,* KOLLE Forlag.

Gummesson, E. (1996) *Towards a Theoretical Framework of Relationship Marketing,* Proceedings of the International Conference on Relationship Marketing, Berlin, pp. 5-18.

Håkansson, H. and Snehota, I. (1995) *Developing Relationships in Business Networks,* Routledge.

Håkansson, H. (1982) *International Marketing and Purchasing of Industrial Goods – An Interaction Approach,* Wiley.

Halinen, A. (1997) *Relationship Marketing in Professional Services – a study of agency-client dynamics in the advertising sector,* Routledge.

Hallén, L. (1984) *Stability and Change in Supplier Relationships.*

Hallén, L. (1994) *Stability and Change in Supplier Relationships.*

Halliburton, C. W. (1994) *Reconciling Global Marketing and 1-to-1 Marketing. A Global Individualism Response,* EMAC

Conference.

Hamel, G. and Prahalad, C. K. (1989) *Strategic Intent*, Harvard Business Review, vol. May-June, pp. 63-76.

Hansen, F. (1972) *Consumer Choice Behaviour. A Cognitive Theor,*. Free Press.

Hayes, H. M., Jenster, P. V. and Aaby, N.-E. (1996*) Business Marketing – A Global Perspective*, Irwin

Hedaa, L. (1991) *On Interorganizational Relationships in Industrial Marketing*, Samfundslitteratur.

Hedaa, L. (1993) *Distrust, Uncertainties and Disconfirmed Expectations in Supplier-Customer Relationships*, International Business Review.

Hedaa, L. (1996) *Customer Acquisition in Sticky Business Markets*. Copenhagen Business School.

Heikkila, J. (1996) *Skanska & Rockwool: Making the supply chain partnership work*, Case IMD.

Heskett, J. L., Jones, T. O., Loveman, G. W., Sasser W., E. Jr., and Schlesinger, L. A. (1994) *Putting the Service profit Chain to Work*, Harvard Business Review, vol. March-April, pp. 164 – 175.

Heskett, J.L.; Sasser, W. et al. (1990) *Service Breakthroughs – Changing the Rules of the Game*, Free Press.

Hill, C. W. L., and Jones, G. R. (1992) *Strategic Management Theory: An Integrated Approach*, Houghton Mifflin Company

Hougaard, S. (1994) *Den Markedsorienterede Virksomhed: En diagnostisk indkredsning af begrebet markedsorientering og dets praktiske anvendelse*, Handelshøjskolen i København.

Hougaard, S. (1995) *Relationstankegang som virksomhedsfilosofi i fremtidens pengeinstitut*. Handelshøjskolen i København.

Hunt, S. D. and Morgan, R. M. (1994) *Relationship marketing in the era of network competition*, Journal of Marketing Management, vol. 5 (5), pp. 18-28.

James, W. and Hatten, K. (1995) *Further evidence on the validity of the self typing paragraph approach; Miles and Snow strategic archetypes in banking*, Strategic Management Journal, vol. 16(2), pp. 161-168.

Jenster, P. V. and Hussey, D. (2001), *Company Analysis – Determining Strategic Capability*, Wiley.

Kelly S. (2000) *Analytical CRM: The fusion of data ad intelligence*, Interactive Marketing.

Kjeldsen, J. (1997) *Køberinitiativ, indkøbsmarketing og leverandørsamarbejde*, Ledelse & Erhvervsøkonomi, vol. 2, pp. 145-157.

Koehn, N. (2001) *Brand New: How entrepreneurs earned Consumer Trust from Wedgeod to Dell,* Harvard Business Scholl Press.

Kohli, A.K. and Jaworski, B.J.(1990) *Market Orientation: The construct, research, propositions and managerial implications*, Journal of Marketing.

Kohli, A.K.and Jaworski, B..J. (1993) *Market orientation: Antecedents and consequences.* Journal of Marketing.

Kotler, P. (1988) *Marketing Management*, Prentice Hall

Kotler, P. (1992) *It's time for Total Marketing*, Business Week Advance Executive Brief, vol. 2.

Kotler, P. (1992) *Total Marketing*, Business Week, Advance Executive Brief no. 2.

Kotler, P. (1997) *Method for the millenium*, Marketing Business, vol. February.

Kotler, P., Armstrong, G., Saunders J.,and Wong V. (1999) *Principals of Marketing*, Prentice Hall.

Krajlik, P. (1983) *Purchasing must become supply management*, Harvard Business Review, SEP-OCT, vol. 61, 5

Kuhn, T. S. (1970) *The Structure of Scientific Revolutions*, University of Chicago Press.

Kunøe, G. (1994) *Metalojalitet*, Working Paper. Handelshøjskolen i Købehavn.

Kurzrock, W. (1996), The Sales Strategist, Irwin

Larreché, J.C. and Gatignon, H. (1990) *Markstrat – A Marketing Management Simulation*, The Scientific Press.

Levitt, T. (1960) *Marketing Myopia*, Harvard Business Review.

Levitt, T. (1983) *After the sale is over.* Harvard Business Review.

Lippert-Rasmussen, M. and Mols, N. P. (1993) *Transaktions-omkostningsteori – en introduktion til Williamson*, Institute of Management University of Aarhus.

MacDonald, M. and Rogers, B. (1998) *Key Account Management*, Butterworth-Heinemann

Macneil, I. (1980) *The New Social Contract, An inquiry into Modern Contractual Relations*, Yale University Press.

Mattson, L. G. (1994) *An Application of Network Approach to Marketing: Defending and Changing Market Positions*, JAI Press Greenwich CT 1985. American Marketing Association.

McDaniel, S. W. and Kolari, J. (1987) *Marketing strategy implications of the Miles and Snow strategic typology*, Journal of Marketing, vol. 51(4), pp. 19-30.

McKenna, R.(1992) *Relationship marketing – win the market through strategic customer relationship*, Century Business.

Menard, C. (ed.) (1997) *Transaction Cost Economics – Recent Developments*, Elgar.

Miles, R. E. and Snow, C. C. (1978) *Organisational Strategy, Structure, and Process*, McGraw-Hill.

Miles, R. E. et al (1988) *Organisational Strategy, Structure, and Process*, in The Strategy Process: Concepts, Context and Cases, Ed. By Quinn, Brian, et al. Prentice Hall, pp. 524-530.

Miller, R. B. and Heiman S. E. (1991) *Successful large account management*, Warner Books.

Millman, T. (1995) *Key Account Management in Business-to-Business Markets*, in A. Payne (ed.) Advances in Relationship Marketing, Kogan Page

Mintzberg, H. and Waters, J. A. (1985) *Of Strategies, Deliberate and Emergent*, Strategic Management Journal, pp. 257-272.

Möller, K. K.E. (1992) *Interorganizational Marketing Exchange: Metatheoretical Analysis of Dominant Research Approaches*, ELASM.

Monthoux de Guillet, P. B.L. (1975) *Organizational Mating*

and Industrial Marketing Conservatism – some Reasons why Industrial Marketing Managers resist Marketing Global Theory, Industrial Marketing Management.

Morgan, R. M. and Hunt, S. D. (1994) *The Commitment-Trust Theory of Relationship Marketing*, Journal of Marketing.

Moriarty, R. T. and Sharpiro, B. P. (1980) *National Account Management*, MSI Report, pp. 80-104.

Moriarty, R. T. and Sharpiro, B. P. (1981) *National Account Management – Emerging Insights*, MSI Report, pp. 82-100.

Moriarty, R. T. and Sharpiro, B. P. (1984) *Organizing the National Account Force*, MSI Report, pp. 84-101.

Nelson, R. R. and Winter, S. (1982) *An Evolutionary Theory of Economic Change*, Harvard University Press.

Nielsen, O. (1995) *Organisationers købsadfærd i grundtræk*, Samfundslitteratur.

Nielsen, O. and Wilke, R. (1999) *Organisationers købsadfærd i grundtræk*, Samfundslitteratur.

Nonaka, I. and Takeuchi, H. (1995) *The Knowledge-Creating Company*, Oxford.

Norman, R. and Ramirez, R. (1983) *From Value Chain to Value Constellation; Designing Interactive Strategy*, Harvard Business Review

Owusu, R. (1997) *Relationship Marketing and the Interaction-inetwork Approach*, Svenska Handelshögskolan i Helsinki.

Palmer A. J. (1996) *Relationship Marketing: A universal Paradigm or Marketing Fad?*, The Learning Organisation.

Pardo, C., Salle, R. and Spencer, R. (1994) *The Key Accountization of the Firm*, Industrial Marketing Management, vol. 22, pp. 123-134.

Parvatiyar, A. (1995) *Evolution of Relational Marketing*, Presentation Paper Emory University for Handelshøjskolen i København.

Parvatiyar, A. and Sheth, J. (1995) *Contemporary Knowledge of Relationship Marketing*, Emory University.

Parvatiyar, A. and Sheth, J. (1995) *Relationship Marketing in Consumer Markets: Antecendents and Consequenses*, Emory

University.

Parvatiyar, A. and Sheth, J. (1995) *Toward a Theory of Relational Partnering Governance,* Presentation Materials Emory University for Meeting in Oslo.

Payne, A. F. (1988) *Developing a Marketing-Oriented Organization*, Business Horizons.

Penrose, E. (1959) *The Theory of The Growth of the Firm*, Basil Blackwell.

Penrose, E. T. (1959) *The Theory of the Growth of the Firm*, Oxford University Press

Peter, J.P and Olson, J.C. (1990) *Consumer Behaviour and Marketing Strategy*, Irwin.

Pfeffer, J. and Salancik, G. R. (1978) *The External Control of Organizations: A Resource Dependence Perspective*, Harper & Row.

Pickton, D. and Broderick, A. (2001) *Integrated Marketing Communication*, Pearson Education.

Pompa N., Berry J. Reid J. and Webber R. (1995) *Relationship Marketing for competitive Advatage: Winning and keeping customers*, Butterworth-Heinemann.

Porter, M. (1980) *Competitive Strategy*, The Free Press.

Porter, M. E. (1982) *Competitive Strategy: Techniques for Analyzing Industries and Competitors,* Free Press.

Porter, M. E. (1985) *Competitive Advantage: Creating and Sustaining Superior Performance*, Free Press.

Porter, M. E. (1990) *The Competitive Advantage of Nations,* Macmillan Press.

Porter, M. E. (2001) *Strategy and the Internet*, Harvard Business Review, vol. March.

Prahalad, C.K. and Hamel, G. (1990) *The Core Competence of the Corporation*, Harvard Business Review.

Prahalad, C.K. and Hamel, G. (1994) *Competing for the Future,* Harvard Business School Press.

Randall, G. (1994) *Trade Marketing Strategies: The partnership between manufacturers, brands and retailers*, Butterworth-Heinemann.

Reichheld, F. (1993) *Loyalty-Based Management*, Harvard Business Review.

Reichheld, F. (1996) *The Quest for Loyalty – Creating Value through Partnership*, Harvard.

Reichheld, F. and Sasser, W..E. jr. (1995) *Zero defections: quality comes to services*, Harvard Business Review.

Reichheld, F. and Schefter, P. (2000) *E-loyalty – your secret weapon on the web*, Harvard Business Review, vol. July-August.

Reichheld, F. and Schefter, P. (2000) *Your secret Weapon*, Harvard Business Review.

Reilly, M. and Parkinson, T. (1985) *Individual and Product Correlates of Evoked Set Size,* Advances in Consumer Research.

Reve, T. (1990) *The Firm as Nexus of Internal and External Contracts from The Firm as a Nexus of Treaties*, in Gustafsson, A. and Williamson, O. E. (eds). Sage Publications.

Robinson, P.J, Faris, C.W. and Wind, Y. (1967) *Industrial Buying and Creative Marketing,* Allyn & Bacon.

Rogers, E. M. and Kincaid, D. L. (1981) *Communication Networks – towards a new paradigm for Research*, The Free Press.

Rottenberger-Murtha, K. (1992) *A NAM by Any Other Name*, Sales and Marketing Management, vol. 144, no. 15, pp. 40-46.

Sawhney, M. and Parikh, D. (2001) *Where Value lives in a networked world?*, Harvard Business Review, vol. January.

Schijns, J.M.C. (1996) *Measuring relationship strenghts for segmentation purposes,* Center for Relationship Marketing,.

Shapiro, R. D. (1985) *Toward Effective Supplier Management: International Comparisons*, Harvard Business School Working Paper.

Skytte, H. (1990) *Interorganisatoriske relationer i vertikale markedsføringssystemer*, Ph.D. dissertation, HHÅ.

Slater, S. F. and Olson, E. M. (2000) *Strategy type and performance: the influence of sales force management*, Strategic Management Journal, vol. 21, pp. 813-829.

Sørensen, C. (1997) *Transaktionsomkostningsteori versus Relationship marketing som paradigme på business-to-business markedet*, IAØ, Handelshøjskolen i København.

Stenvinkel Nilsson, O. and Olsen, J. K. (1969) *En adfærdste-oretisk model til beregning af kunders levetid og værdi*, Handelshøjskolen i København.

Stern, L. W. and El-Ansary, A. I. (1992) *Marketing Channels*, Fifth Edition, Prentice Hall.

Stern, L. W. and Reve, T. (1980) *Distribution Channels as Political Economies: A Framework for Comparative Analysis*, Journal of Marketing, vol. 44, pp. 52-64.

Storbacka, K. (1993) *Customer Relationship in Retail Banking*, Helsinki.

Svanholmer, B. (1996) *Kundeloyalitet*, Børsens Forlag.

Sviokla, John J. and Shapiro, B. (1993) *Seeking Customers*, Harvard Business School Press.

Tanskanen, K. (1994) *Supplier Management in Just-in-time Manufacturing*, Acta Polytechnica Scandinavia, The Finnish Academy of Technology.

Thompson, J. D. (1973) *Hur organisationer fungerar*, Bokförlaget Prisma.

Tollin, K. (1990) *Konsumentbilder i Marknadsföringen av Livsmedel*, Stockholms Universitet, Akademitryck.

Turnbull, P.W and Valla, J. P. (1986): *Strategies for International Industrial Marketing: the Management of Customer Relationships in European Industrial Markets,* Croom Helm.

Turnbull, P.W. and Valla, J. P. (1992) *Strategies for International Industrial Marketing,* Croom Helm.

Uncles, M. (1994) *Do Your Customers need a loyalty scheme?*, Journal of Targeting, Measurement and Analysis.

Williamson, O. E. (1975) *Markets and Hierarchies – Analysis and Antitrust Implications*, The Free Press.

Williamson, O. E. (1985) *The Economic Institutions of Capitalism – Firms, Markets, Relational Contracting*, Free Press.

Zahra, S. and Pearce, J. (1990) *Research evidence on the Miles-Snow Typology*, Journal of Management, vol. 16(4), pp. 751-768.

Index